THE
LONELY HOUSE

STRENGTH FOR TIMES OF LOSS
NEW REVISED AND ENLARGED EDITION

LOWELL O. ERDAHL

C.S.S. Publishing Co.
Lima, Ohio

LIBRARY OF CONGRESS
Cataloging-in-Publication Data

Erdahl, Lowell O.
  The lonely house : strength for times of loss / by Lowell O. Erdahl.
— New, rev., enl. ed.
      p.   cm.
  ISBN 1-556-73117-5
  1. Consolation. I. Title.
BV4905.2.E73   1989   88-28304
242'.4—dc19   CIP

Second Printing **1989**
Third Printing 1991
Fourth Printing **1992**

Copyright © 1989 by
The C.S.S. Publishing Company, Inc.
Lima, Ohio

Scripture quotations unless otherwise noted are from the Revised Standard Version Common Bible, copyrighted © 1973.

Scripture quotations noted NEB are from the New English Bible, copyright © the Delegates of the Oxford University Press and the Syndics of the Cambridge University Press, 1961, 1970.

Lines on page 107 are from "A Shropshire Lad" — Authorised Edition — from *The Collected Poems of A. E. Housman*. Copyright 1939, 1940, © 1965 by Holt, Rinehart and Winston. Copyright © 1967, 1968 by Robert E. Symons. Reprinted by permission of Holt, Rinehart and Winston, Publishers. Also by permission of the Society of Authors as the literary representatives of the Estate of A. E. Housman; and Jonathon Cape Ltd., publishers of A. E. Housman's *Collected Poems*.

Lines on page 108 are from Stephen Vincent Benet's poem "Thirty-Five" published by Holt, Rinehart and Winston.

9828 / ISBN 1-55673-117-5   PRINTED IN U.S.A.

To the memory of my parents
Chris and Inga Erdahl,
whose love and wisdom sustain me still

Preface

This book is for people who know what it is like to be "bowed down with grief." I did not know the meaning of that phrase until a freakish bolt of lightning ended the life of our 25-year-old son. In the days that followed, my body would often be bowed with racking sobs. I discovered what so many others have come to know — the loss of a child is exceedingly painful and heart-rending.

Grief over the loss of a loved one ushers a person into a new and unwanted world of experiences. One enters, as it were, a forest full of uncharted trails. Each fresh realization of the loss, with its unsettling emotional dynamics, forces one to walk down yet another uncharted path.

The emotions which follow a loss experience are often puzzling. There may be anger that shows itself in a feisty spirit; there may be guilt over any small omission; there may be a preoccupation which makes it difficult to concentrate on matters at hand. In addition, the mind wants answers to the question "Why?" and the heart asks for some way of communicating again with the loved person now gone.

Because most of us are strangers to grief, we hunger for whatever can give direction, information or counsel. I, for one, found myself devouring every letter, every card, every book, every verse that was sent me. I spent weeks of hours looking up every passage in my Bible that speaks of angels, death, heaven, the life to come.

These emotions, questions and uncertainties make *The Lonely House* a source of comfort. Questions and answers are handled in a sympathetic and reasonable way. More importantly, each page points toward the resource that can bring healing and strength — the Holy Scriptures and Jesus Christ, who is the focus of these Scriptures.

> Dr. Merton Strommen, Executive Director
> Search Institute and Center for
> Youth & Family Ministry
> Augsburg College
> Minneapolis, Minnesota

Introduction
to the original edition

This book is intended especially for those who have suffered the loss of a person. Among these are the widow and widower; grieving parents and children; other family and friends; the separated and divorced and their children; heartsick survivors of broken love; parents stunned by the stillness of the empty nest; the homesick who grieve the loss of both place and people; the retired, disabled, and unemployed who mourn for companions still at work.

Millions more mourn the loss of health, youth, limbs, money, or work. Hopes and dreams, as well as people, live and die. Some of these "deaths" can be as painful as the loss of a person. Although we shall focus on grief following separation from persons, others, suffering similar losses or seeking to understand another person's bereavement, may also find meaning in these pages.

The daily readings deal with aspects of a theme for each week. They are intended as daily devotionals, but can also be read in weekly sections or straight through, as the reader prefers. Since mourning often lasts much longer than the fifteen weeks that these readings cover, some may wish to use portions of them over again.

It is awesome to think of the realities of life and death, bereavement and bewilderment, loss and loneliness to which we now turn our attention. If you are recently bereaved, these months may be among the most difficult times of your life. No one can do much to lift that burden from you, but in the grace of God we are offered his presence and promises, which enable us to face and feel our loss and to begin to live again.

*The original edition provided readings for fifteen weeks. The revised edition has been expanded to sixteen weeks.

Introduction to the Revised Edition

The first edition of *The Lonely House* was published in 1977 and is now out of print. Many have expressed regret that it is no longer available and have asked for a new edition. In response to their requests, the entire volume has been reviewed and revised. There are at least minor changes on almost every page and much that is new has been added including an entire week of readings on "Decision Making."

From the author's obviously subjective perspective the daily readings have been significantly improved. It is my hope that they will help to sustain and renew the faith, hope and love of many who suffer the pains of loss.

The Lonely House

After Mother died, we visited the old farmhouse where Dad was living alone. When leaving, our daughter, Becky, then five years old, suggested that we should give the house a name. "What should we name it?" we asked. She answered, "We should call it the lonely house."

In those few hours of visiting with her grieving grandfather and roaming the house where she would never again see her grandmother's smile, hear her voice, or feel the touch of her hand, Becky sensed that we had all experienced a great loss.

The old farmhouse is now more lonely still. Dad, too, has died; and, except for visitors, no voice is heard within its walls. That lonely house has become, for us, a symbol of the experience of loss that comes sooner or later to all who live.

We cannot escape occasions of loss, but there are better and worse ways of responding to them. Some lead to healing and renewal of life, others to greater loss of health and of hope. We seek in these pages to find the better ways.

Prayer: O Lord, keep us through times of loss and lead us to new beginnings. In Jesus' name. Amen

Thought for the day: Loss comes to all who live.

"Nobody Can Take His Place"

Genesis 1:26-31

In a former parish, seminary student interns had responsibility for youth work. I once introduced a new intern to a high school student saying, "I would like you to meet Tom Duke. He's taking Wendell Friest's place." To which the high school student replied, "Nobody can take his place."

That student was right; no one ever takes another person's place. We may carry on another's work and complete what someone else has begun, but we do not take another's place. We are all created "in the image of God" (Genesis 1:27) but none of us is exactly the same as any other person. Each of us is a unique human being with a special place in our world and in the lives of the people with whom we live.

If we do not realize that fact before, it is forced upon us when death or similar separation take us apart. Other people, of course, keep and take their places in our lives. But none of them fills the empty place left by the person who is no longer with us. That void remains as a painful reminder of the special significance of the person who is no longer with us.

Prayer: Thank you, Lord, for our individuality. Make us the persons we alone can be and keep us mindful of the uniqueness of others. In Jesus' name. Amen

Thought for the day: Each of us has a place no other can fill.

Week One   Luke 16:19-31
Day Three   *God Leaves It Empty*   Exodus 20:1-3

The death or departure of someone who has had a special place in our lives leaves a void no other person can fill. God could no doubt fill that place. He could move in and so fill the void that we would never miss the person again. God could, but he does not. As if in tribute to the unique worth and significance of that person, he leaves the place empty.

In the anguish of living with that empty place, it may seem as if God too is gone. The absence of the person we loved may seem a sign of the absence of God. When this happens, our feelings deceive us. God does not fill the empty place, but he seeks to take his own place in our lives. He remains God for us, inviting us to trust his love and power and promising us to keep us in his grace. To live in trust of the goodness of God has an effect on everything we think and do, but it does not free us from the experience of grieving. Secure in God's love we dare to face the reality of our loss and feel the full pain of it.

Prayer: O Lord our God, be God for us in love and power. We take our places as people and let you take your place as God. In Jesus' name. Amen

Thought for the day: God takes his own, but no one else's place.

God Lets Us
Feel the Loss

John 11:33-35

God does not fill the empty place; nor does he rush in to wipe away our tears or heal our broken hearts. That we too may pay tribute to the departed person, he lets us feel the pain of loss. That pain is the price we pay for having loved and having let someone love us. Could it be any other way? The pain of parting is a measure of what a person meant to us.

The shock of death or separation may leave us numb and unable to feel anything. This is not a sign of lack of love, but a built-in anesthetic that lets us survive. As numbness passes, the pain of parting makes itself felt. Beyond this pain is healing, and we hope for the day when "he will wipe away every tear from their eyes, and death shall be no more, neither shall there be mourning nor crying nor pain any more." (Revelation 21:4) But this joy is not now. Neither broken bones nor broken hearts heal quickly. We give God time to do his healing work and seek neither to rush nor to prolong it.

Prayer: Dear God, thank you for the capacity to love and to grieve. Give us strength to love and strength to grieve, and heal us through it all. In Jesus' name. Amen

Thought for the day: To grieve is to have loved and been loved.

Reality or Nightmare?

Some losses are so sudden or tragic that it is extremely difficult for us to comprehend or accept them. We may have thought we were ready, but it is doubtful that we can ever be fully prepared. When we first visited the lonely house after Mother's death, there were times when we would catch ourselves looking up to see if she were the person coming through the door. We knew she was no longer there; her death was clear in our minds, but something in us refused to believe it. An inner voice of longing cried out, "Come back, come back." Our minds knew this could not be, but our hearts still hoped all this was but a tragic dream.

The suddenness of Mother's death made it especially difficult to accept; but others tell us that, sudden or not, ours was not a novel experience. When shaken by loss, we wonder, Is this reality or nightmare? As Job learned, some trouble is too much to bear. We cannot quickly take it in. This may be well; were we to feel it all at once, we might burn out like a 12-volt bulb in a 220-volt socket. It can take months to face and feel the pain of tragic loss.

Prayer: Thank you, Lord, for our protective defenses. Give us love to be patient with ourselves and others. In Jesus' name. Amen

Thought for the day: It takes time to face and feel our losses.

14

To stand by the deathbed of a loved one, to place a hand on the cold, folded hands, to receive the final decree of divorce or notice of termination of employment, to hear the doctor say, "There is nothing more we can do," can send tremors of terror through our souls. But these also bring us face to face with painful reality.

There are unnecessary and un-Christian funeral practices involving elaborate and expensive burial rights. But there is also ancient wisdom in having a time of visitation and reviewal when family and friends can meet in the presence of death. During the funeral it is well that the casket be closed but there is often wisdom in having it open during the visitation. Seeing the dead can help us face and accept the reality of death.

As we are grateful for the way in which a Christian funeral can help us experience and endure the grief that comes with death, we also seek means of helping one another through other losses that may be equally severe and for which no similar help is provided. When a romance breaks up, the loss may be as painful as the death of a parent, yet the only "comfort" received from family and friends may be jesting comments about "other fish in the sea." People usually show compassion toward grief over divorce, separation, the empty nest, retirement, or a family move; but such mourning is often a lonely business.

Prayer: O Lord, give us courage to face and feel our losses, and compassion to care for others who grieve. Amen

Thought for the day: In Christ we are the cared for and the caring.

Week One　　　　　　　*From*　　　　　Romans 6:3-4
Day Seven　　　*Death to Life*　2 Corinthians 5:16-21

The reality of loss comes home to us through the absence of the person we have lost. We wander alone through the silent house, look across the table to an empty chair, sleep alone in a lonely bed, face the day dreaming of colleagues with whom we no longer share the challenge of daily work, have no one with whom to make decisions and help plan the day — all these tell us that life will never be the same again.

But they do not say that life will never be meaningful again. God, who has given us capacity to love and to grieve, has also built into us capacities for renewal and rebirth. By his power we can be raised to "walk in newness of life." (Romans 6:4) But that will be a new life, not a return to the old life.

In the grace of God, life is a continuous adventure out of the old and into the new, out of the past and into the future. In Christ our failures and tragedies are not final. "If anyone is in Christ, he is a new creation; the old has passed away, behold the new has come." (2 Corinthians 5:17) God has the last word and in Christ we dare believe that this word is not death, but life.

Prayer: Lead us, O Lord, through our times of loss into newness of life. In Jesus' name. Amen

Thought for the day: Our hope is not in return, but in renewal.

Promises For
Terrible Times

God's promises seek to sustain us through this terrible time. Paul says, "Grace to you and peace from God our Father and the Lord Jesus Christ." (Romans 1:7) This is more than a greeting: it promises the love and power of God to all who trust him. Paul saw our sufferings and sorrows not as signs of the absence of God's love, but as reminders of the sufferings of Christ in whom we have the assurance of God's love and power in every circumstance.

Paul's word of grace to Christians, then, is also his word to us who suffer now. He says in effect: "You have suffered a great loss — perhaps even loss of faith in God. You have many reasons for doubting God's presence and disbelieving his love. But remember the suffering of Christ and God's promise of grace to you in him. God loves you now and will love you forever. Remembering Jesus, dare to trust that nothing that has or can ever happen will stop God from loving you."

Prayer: Thank you, God, for your grace to us in Christ. Give us faith to trust you now. In Jesus' name. Amen

Thought for the day: We cannot stop God from loving us.

God Shares
Our Suffering

When sorrow tempts us to doubt God's grace, we remember that the supreme revelation of God's love comes from a place of suffering and death. Through Christ on the Cross, we see into the heart of God. Then we dare trust that God is with us in our suffering, feeling in his own heart the pain of our grief.

Christ, the "man of sorrows, and acquainted with grief" (Isaiah 53:3), reaches out to touch our lives. Jesus invites us to trust that we do not suffer alone; God suffers too, feeling in his heart the anguish in our lives.

Some think God is beyond all suffering, but in Jesus we see a God so great in love that he shares in all the suffering of creation. The Cross reminds us of the suffering of the world; but more than that, the Cross of Christ assures us that our pains are God's pain and our sorrows God's sorrow.

Prayer: O God, give us courage to trust that you share our sorrows and feel the pain of our suffering. In Jesus' name. Amen

Thought for the day: I feel some of the world's suffering; God feels it all.

"For Thou Art With Me" Psalm 23:1-6
Psalm 46:1-11

Centuries ago the psalmist wrote, "Even though I walk through the valley of the shadow of death, I fear no evil; for thou art with me." (Psalm 23:4) His hope was not in the absence of trouble, but in the presence of God. So also for us. God has not promised to spare us all trouble, but he has promised always to be with us. Now as then, "God is our refuge and strength, a very present help in trouble." (Psalm 46:1)

Some think it wrong to "use God" in times of trouble, and we can wrongly do so. But part of the good news is that God lets us use him. Held in God's love through terrible times, we are healed and made useful again. Even after we have turned aside from him, he remains a refuge in whom we can trust again.

Julian of Norwich said, "God has not promised that you will never be tempted, troubled or distressed; but God has promised that you will never be overcome." This, too, is our trust in every time of trouble.

Prayer: O Lord, thank you for the promise of your abiding presence. Be for us our refuge and our strength in this and every time of trouble. Amen

Thought for the day: God lets us use him so that he may increase our usefulness to others.

Week Two   *"I Will Never*   Hebrews 13:5-6
Day Four   *Fail You"*   Matthew 27:45-50
    Luke 23:44-49

We fail ourselves and fail one another. But God has promised, "I will never fail you nor forsake you." (Hebrews 13:5) When feelings of forsakenness threaten to overwhelm us, we remember that Jesus has been this way before us. In suffering on the Cross, Jesus cried, "My God, my God, why hast thou forsaken me?" (Matthew 27:46) This cry was not a sin needing forgiveness. These words express the honest anguish of all who feel forsaken, and they free us also to cry to God in our troubles.

As we do so, we realize that Jesus' cry was a prayer and that he went on to pray: "Father, into thy hands I commit my spirit." (Luke 23:46) Gerhard Frost has said that these words "teach us everything we need to know about how to die." They also teach us how to live and how to grieve, trusting that, however we feel, God's promise still holds true: "I will never fail you nor forsake you."

Prayer: Though feeling forsaken, we still cry to you, O Lord; hear our prayer and renew our trust and hope. In Jesus' name. Amen

Thought for the day: Our faith is not based on our feelings but on God's promises.

Death confronts us with the limits of life. Perhaps we once considered ourselves to be strong, but now we know better. Paul Tournier says that it is wrong to divide people into "the strong" and "the weak," for the fact is that we are all weak. In times of tragic loss, we all feel helpless. These feelings are truthful reminders that much of life and death is beyond our control.

But even when helpless, we can still do something. We can turn to the promises of God and trust in him. "Set your troubled hearts at rest," says Jesus. "Trust in God always; trust also in me." (John 14:1 NEB) *Always* is a little word, but it includes this and every moment. When there is nothing else to do, we can still trust in God who "so loved the world that he gave his only Son, that whoever believes in him should not perish but have eternal life." (John 3:16) Take these words to heart. Trust God now; trust God always!

Prayer: O God, thank you for promises that invite our trust. Looking to Jesus, we set our hearts at rest and rely on your love. In Jesus' name. Amen

Thought for the day: When we can do nothing else, we can still trust in God.

Week Two	*"My Grace Is*	2 Cor. 1:8-11
Day Six	*Sufficient For You"*	2 Cor. 12:1-10

When we are weakened by loss, just getting out of bed can be hard work. It may have taken effort to pick up this book. We long for strength to face the duties of the day and the darkness of the night.

When weak in ourselves, we remember Paul's experience: "We were so utterly, unbearably crushed that we despaired of life itself. Why, we felt we had received the sentence of death." But this was not the end of the story: "That was to make us rely not on ourselves but on God who raises the dead; he delivered us from so deadly a peril, and he will deliver us; on him we have set our hope that he will deliver us again." (2 Corinthians 1:8-10)

In his struggles with some kind of affliction, Paul experienced weakness and received this promise: "My grace is sufficient for you, for my power is made perfect in weakness." (2 Corinthians 12:9) Weak in himself, Paul found his strength in God. Strong in our own strength, we are weak; weak in ourselves, we can be strong in God.

Prayer: When we are incapable of anything, enable us, O Lord, to live by your promises and power. In Jesus' name. Amen

Thought for the day: Weak in ourselves, we find our strength in God.

Week Two   Romans 8:31-39
Day Seven   *"If God Be For Us"*   2 Corinthians 1:15-22

After a great loss we often feel that everyone and everything is against us. These feelings reflect some truth; there are anti-life forces at work in the world. But Paul invites us to trust that "God is for us." (Romans 8:31) "The thief comes only to steal and kill and destroy." But, Jesus says, "I came that they may have life, and have it abundantly." (John 10:10) Others may condemn us, and we may condemn ourselves; but God still loves and forgives us.

In Jesus Christ, God speaks a great "Yes" to each of our lives, assuring us of his love and of our worth to him. "As surely as God is faithful, our word to you has not been Yes and No. For the Son of God, Jesus Christ, whom we preached among you . . . was not Yes and No; but in him it is always Yes. For all the promises of God find their Yes in him." (2 Corinthians 1:18-20)

Looking to Jesus, we dare to trust "that neither death, nor life, nor angels, nor principalities, nor things present, nor things to come, nor powers, nor height, nor depth, nor anything else in all creation, will be able to separate us from the love of God in Christ Jesus our Lord." (Romans 8:38-39)

Prayer: Thank you, God, for being for us now and for promising to be with us, and for us, forever. Amen

Thought for the day: God is on the side of life — life in fulness!

Day One   *"A Time To Mourn"*

We have thought of the experience of loss and of God's promises that invite our trust. This week we consider the feelings of grief and depression that usually come with loss.

Normal grief is a form of depression experienced in response to loss. There are sick depressions that result from malfunctions of mind or body, but there are also healthy depressions that are normal reactions to depressing situations. It is no more sick to be depressed with sorrow than to be elated with joy.

There is no virtue in pretending to be happy when we are sad. We are to be honest from the inside out. When we are depressed, it is best to admit it — to ourselves, to at least one other person, and above all to God — not as a sin to be confessed, but as a reality with which we have to deal. There is, as Scripture says, "a time to mourn." (Ecclesiastes 3:4)

Prayer: O Lord, thank you for enabling us to feel both joy and sorrow. Give us healthy mourning. In Jesus' name. Amen

Thought for the day: Tragic events create normal depression.

Time To Do Nothing

When depressed and grieving, we often feel like doing nothing. We could stay in bed all day and sleep or gaze at the ceiling. In our hyperactive society such times may seem an utter waste, but they are really occasions for remembering that it is sometimes all right to do nothing but rest and be passive.

Jesus was not always active. He often went apart to a quiet place of rest and renewal. When Jesus heard of the death of John the Baptizer, "he withdrew from there in a boat to a lonely place apart." (Matthew 14:13) In our grief we also need times of solitude and rest. Martin Luther could speak of faith as pure passivity. Having faith is an act of becoming and being passive. Faith is resting in God's care and letting God hold and love us. While still in bed and doing nothing, we can remember that God holds us as does our bed. We let down the full weight of our loss upon him, trusting that God cares for us. Passive in trust, we let God be active in love.

Prayer: O Lord, we let go of ourselves and rest our lives upon your promised presence. Hold us now and forever. Amen

Thought for the day: When we cease to struggle, we begin to rest in God's love.

Times To Do
Something

We are to be constantly at rest in the love of God. As noted earlier, Jesus invites us to "set your troubled hearts at rest; trust in God always." (John 14:1 NEB) This means that we are to continually rest in the mercy and strength of God, just as a ship rests upon the sea.

But a ship not only rests, it also works, not to hold itself up, but to deliver the passengers and cargo to their destination. Luther stressed that Christian living involves both passive trust and active loving. While passively at rest in the love of God, we are to be actively at work loving people.

One person we are to love is ourselves; and when we are grieving, one way of loving ourselves is to follow a daily ritual of physical activity. In olden days the widows and widowers found some release from sorrow through scrubbing floors and chopping wood. If there is physical work to do, we should do it. If not, a long walk or a period of vigorous exercise each day helps break the depression and revive our strength. When we don't feel like doing it we are to do it anyway. It is one way of fulfilling God's command to love ourselves and it helps to revive our strength so that we can love others.

Prayer: Enable us, O Lord, to do what we should even when we don't feel like doing it. In Jesus' name. Amen

Thought for the day: At rest in God, we act in love.

"Jesus wept" (John 11:35), and, with those tears, Jesus assures us that it is right to cry in times of loss. Tears and laughter are unique human gifts. When something is funny, it is good to laugh; and, when sad it is good to cry. Many men especially need assurance from Jesus, the most manly of men, that times of loss are times for tears.

Some cry easily and often, others seldom, if at all. Some do not like to cry in public, but are able to cry freely when alone. We should not feel forced to cry; nor should we let social pressure or personal inhibition keep us from the tears we feel like shedding.

When stunned by loss, we may be unable to cry. We may be surprised that a sentimental story or memory moves us to tears while a great loss does not. If so, we can let such little sentimentalities help free us to weep for the greater loss. Little by little, as we are able to express it through words, deeds, and tears, the intensity of grief ebbs away and the mood of depression begins to lift.

Prayer: Thank you, Lord, for laughter and tears. When things are funny, free us to laugh. When they are sad, free us to cry. In Jesus' name, Amen

Thought for the day: Both tears and laughter are God's gifts for our good.

Week Three   *It's Sad To*   Acts 20:31-38
Day Five   *Say Good-bye*

Times of parting are often times of tears. When Paul said good-bye to his friends, "they all wept." (Acts 20:37)

It's sad to say good-bye. We part with friends, wondering if we will meet again. Retirement parties may be times of jokes and laughter, but they are also sad occasions. When a marriage ends in divorce, feelings of relief often merge with sorrow. Saddest of all are the partings brought by death.

When loved ones die, we say good-bye to them one at a time. How sad this is only the bereaved can tell. When we die, we say good-bye to all our loved ones at one time. How sad this is only the dying can tell.

Even when we are sustained by God's promises so that we are not afraid to die, it is still sad to say good-bye. Every loss reminds us of the limits of life, and in our sorrows we grieve also for our own deaths and for the immense sadness that is part of each day's dying.

Prayer: Thank you, Lord, for life so good we hate to see it end. Thank you, too, for promise of life beyond our dying. Amen

Thought for the day: Glad hellos are followed by sad good-byes, except for this: we need never say good-bye to God.

We Do Not Grieve Alone

In times of loss we often feel desperately alone. It may seem as if everyone else is happy while we alone are sad. These feelings are understandable but false. At this moment millions grieve over losses of a thousand kinds.

If we are so many, need we all suffer alone? Can we help one another endure our sorrow and come through our grief? Many are doing so already. Most such help is given in informal ways, as friends, family, church, and community come together to support and share. Specific assistance is offered by groups like We Care, Parents Without Partners, and Emotions Anonymous, that seek to help people in trouble help each another.

Every experience of loss puts us in need of understanding and help, but it also helps us to understand and enables us to be of help to others. If there is no grief support group in your community explore the possibility of starting one.

Prayer: Lord God, as we need help, give us willingness to receive it. As we can be of help, give us the willingness and the wisdom to give it. Amen

Thought for the day: I need others, and others need me.

We Share
Our Troubles

Paul Tournier believed that we often give more help
to others by confessing our defeats and troubles than by
telling of our victories and joys. Jess Lair has said that "the
most loving thing we can do is tell it like it is with us in
our deepest hearts." If they are right, each of us has great
potential for helpfulness.

The Apostle Paul never heard of Tournier or Lair, but
he did confess his defeats and troubles, and he certainly
told what was in his deepest heart — including the guilt
of his sin and the pain of his sufferings. By doing so, he
has helped millions across the centuries. Paul's example
invites us to tell of our troubles and struggles as well as
our joys.

James says, "Confess your sins to one another and
pray for one another, that you may be healed." (James
5:16) We fear such vulnerability and need to remember
that to love is to be vulnerable. Such self-giving love is a
means of mutual helpfulness and healing. When vulnerable in love, we support and strengthen each other.

Prayer: Thank you, God, for Jesus, in whom you
open your heart to us. Free us also to open our hearts.
In Jesus' name. Amen

Thought for the day: Our problems and pains
give us potential for helpfulness to others.

"Terror On Every Side!"

Psalm 31:1-18

The only thing we have to fear is *not* fear itself. When loss shatters our security there may be "terror on every side." (Psalm 31:13) We may dread being alone, fear losing control, and wonder if we are going crazy. Although exhausted, we may not be sleepy. Through anxious nights we may wonder how to face the coming days. Can we manage financially? What if we get sick? What if we die? What will become of us?

A car stops, the doorbell rings, and for a moment we wonder if he or she is coming back. It is a crazy thought. There will be no coming back. Sometimes we sense a presence and wonder who is there. Are we going crazy? We can't concentrate. Memories roll over in our minds. How can we go on like this? Everything seems to be giving way, and we are anxious and afraid.

Prayer: O Lord, what is happening to us? You promise safety and peace. Help us; we need you now. In Jesus' name. Amen

Thought for the day:
When all around my soul gives way,
He then is all my hope and stay.
On Christ the solid rock, I stand;
All other ground is sinking sand.

The kinds of fears we thought of yesterday are a normal part of many grief experiences. As numbness passes and reality sinks in, we discover that the structure of our lives has been shattered. No wonder we are anxious! This is not a sign that we are going crazy, but a normal reaction to a terrible blow. Even sensing, or fleetingly seeming to see or hear, the departed person is common and no great cause for alarm.

Some people do break down under the stress of grief, and it is well to be aware of danger signals. Like body temperature, the "fever" of grief should be neither too high nor too low. If we are totally out of control, the grief temperature may be too high; if there is a total absence of any feeling, it may be too low. When such conditions persist, a professional evaluation may be in order.

Medications are gifts of God, but they should be taken only as absolutely necessary and discontinued as soon as possible. We have enough problems without developing an unhealthy dependence on chemicals, and need especially beware of medicating ourselves with alcohol and other drugs. It is frightening to face a loss, but there is no healthy escape from doing so.

Prayer: O Lord, give us courage to endure the normal anxieties of loss. When we need help, guide us to find it. Amen

Thought for the day: Anxiety is normal to those who grieve.

At Rest
In The Storm

"A great storm of wind arose, and the waves beat into the boat," and yet Jesus was "asleep on the cushion." (Mark 4:37, 38) When waves of anxiety threaten to swamp our little boats, we wish for peace in the midst of the storm.

Jesus promises that kind of peace — not negative peace from the absence of trouble, but a positive peace from the presence of God. To "all who labor and are heavy laden" Jesus says, "Come to me . . . and I will give you rest." (Matthew 11:28) Again he says, "Set your troubled hearts at rest. Trust in God always; trust also in me." (John 14:1, NEB)

In Christ, God invites us to rest securely in his arms of strong and tender love. Whatever our age, Christ calls us to live with the confidence of which many of us once learned and still love to sing:

> Children of the heavenly Father
> Safely in his bosom gather;
> Nestling bird nor star in heaven
> Such a refuge e'er was given.
> Neither life nor death shall ever
> From the Lord his children sever . . .

Prayer: In the storms of life we find our peace in your presence, O Lord. Hold us now and keep us forever. In Jesus' name. Amen

Thought for the day: Our peace comes not from the absence of trouble but from the presence of God.

Peace Beyond Understanding

Having been shocked by terror, we may also be surprised by peace. We look back over dreadful days and marvel to have survived them at all. Even now, we may sense a place of peace within our hearts.

In such moments we begin to understand what Paul meant by "the peace of God, which passes all understanding." (Philippians 4:7) We do not *attain* this peace; it is not the result of our struggle and striving. *We obtain* it as the gift of God. It comes from Christ, who stands guard over our lives. All we can do is "let go, and let God." As our prayers turn from anxious pleading to restful yielding, we let God keep our hearts and minds in Christ Jesus. Then the Prince of Peace reigns in our lives and in the safety of his care lines of an old hymn take on new meaning:

> Peace to sooth our bitter woes
> God in Christ on us bestows . . .
> Peace be with you, full and free
> Now and through eternity.

Prayer: O Prince of Peace, rule now in our anxious lives. Cleanse us of foolish fears and give us courage to face the real ones. In your name. Amen

Thought for the day: I let go, and let God give me peace.

Sleep In Safety

Insomnia is common to many who grieve. Though tense and tired we may fail to feel sleepy and, when we do doze off, we may waken a little later, still restless and fatigued. The harder we try to sleep, the more sleep eludes us.

In sleepless hours we are again reminded that some things cannot be done by our trying to do them. A child tries to catch a butterfly; but run as he will, it is beyond his grasp. When he gives up and kneels in the meadow, the butterfly may land on his shoulder.

So, too, with sleep. It comes as a gift of grace. We cannot achieve it, but we can cease the feverish quest that drives it away. Remember that we rest without sleeping and that we can survive many a sleepless night. Having consented to stay awake, we may be surprised to fall asleep.

Sleeping pills may be a blessing but, like other drugs, should be taken only as necessary. When we are wakeful, one safe thing is to feed our minds with thoughts like this: "In peace I will both lie down and sleep; for thou alone, O Lord, makest me dwell in safety." (Psalm 4:8)

Prayer: O Lord, even when sleepless we rest in the safety of your care. In Jesus' name. Amen

Thought for the day: I will trust, but not try, to sleep.

Week Four   *One Day*   Matthew 6:24-34
Day Six   *At A Time*   2 Corinthians 6:1-2

We can usually manage today; it is tomorrow that we dread. We long for strength today to face all our tomorrows. But God does not provide lifelong strength in a single day. As we live one breath and one heartbeat at a time, so God gives us grace moment by moment.

Jesus invites us to live one day at a time: "Do not be anxious about tomorrow . . . Let the day's own trouble be sufficient for the day." (Matthew 6:34) As we greet each new day, we are promised, "As your days, so shall your strength be." (Deuteronomy 33:25) In Christ we trust there will never be a time when God will fail to supply strength for that day. Whatever happens, God will be there with grace sufficient for our need.

If one day at a time is too long, we can divide it into hours, minutes, and moments. As grace comes moment by moment, we can learn to live one moment, one breath, one heartbeat at a time.

Prayer: O Lord, forgive us for wanting a lifetime of strength in every hour. Thank you for your presence now. In this moment we live by grace. In Jesus' name. Amen

Thought for the day: We live in neither the past nor the future. We live now and *now* is the moment of grace!

God Will Bring Us Through

When we doubt our ability to carry on, Paul speaks to our need: "I am sure that he who began a good work in you will bring it to completion at the day of Jesus Christ." (Philippians 1:6)

We did not choose to be here and, on some days, may wish we never had been born. But here we are, alive in a world abounding in anguish. In spite of all our troubles, Jesus invites us to believe that God has begun a good work in us. His grace has brought us through the joys and sorrows of the past and, though we may feel unable to go on from here, God promises to enable us to carry on.

In Christ we dare to trust that someday we will know the full peace of his victory over death and every evil. In the meantime, we venture each day, assured that God will not bring us to any place where his grace will not keep us.

Prayer: Thank you, Lord, for power to see us through. Bring to completion the good work you have begun in us. In Jesus' name. Amen

Thought for the day:
Through many dangers, toils and snares,
I have already come;
'Tis grace hath brought me safe thus far,
And grace will lead me home.

The Anguish
Of Regret

Among the most universal emotions at times of loss are feelings of regret. "Why didn't I call the doctor sooner?" "I should have driven myself!" "How could I have said such terrible things?" "Why didn't we talk about it?" "If only I had realized . . ." "How could I have been so stupid?" "Why did I . . .?" "Why didn't I . . .?" Such memories often come rushing back to convict us of sins of comission and omission; and, at fault or not, we still feel terrible and have to deal with this anguish of regret.

In the safety of God's love, we are given courage to be honest with ourselves and others. Sometimes we must honestly say, "I made a terrible mistake!" On other occasions the truth is, "It's not my fault!" We need forgiveness, but we must also realize that we have no monopoly on mistakes and are not personally to blame for every wrong.

Prayer: O Lord, give us honesty to face our failures and grace to triumph over them. In Jesus' name. Amen

Thought for the day: All who live, must deal with regret.

Inappropriate Feelings 1 John 3:19-24
                        Of Guilt

The rest of this week we shall consider feelings of guilt that are an honest response to actual failure. But today we shall think about guilt feelings not founded in failure. When we have sinned, we need forgiveness; when we have not sinned, but still feel guilty, we need to bring our feelings in line with reality.

A husband is killed on the way to the post office to mail a package for his wife. She blames herself. Had she gone instead, he would not have died. True, but she did not cause his death. He was not a child to be guided by the hand. He may have been careless, or another driver, or both, may have been at fault.

We cannot protect loved ones from all danger, nor should we blame ourselves for wrongs caused by others. Having enough sins of our own, we need not feel guilty for the failures of others.

There are also events over which we rightly feel sad but for which we should not feel guilty. A friend told of an agonizing decision: "I don't feel bad for what I did," he said, "but I feel terrible for having had to do it." Such are some of life's choices. A wise and tragically necessary divorce, for example, may leave a couple in grief but they should not feel guilty for having done the right thing.

Prayer: Save us, O Lord, from improper guilt feelings. Give us wisdom to take responsibility for our lives and to let others take responsibility for theirs. In Jesus' name. Amen

Thought for the day: I am responsible for my behavior and not the behavior of others.

Week Five   Psalm 32:1-11
Day Three   *When We Are At Fault*   Luke 18:9-14
                                              Romans 3:9-20

What if guilt feelings are in order? We were at fault. Our carelessness caused injury. We should have called the doctor. Unkind words should never have been spoken. Words of kindness and deeds of love should have been said and done. Perhaps a life, a marriage, a friendship, might have been saved; but now it is too late.

What's done is done and there is nothing we or anyone else can do about it. "All the king's horses and all the king's men couldn't put Humpty Dumpty together again." Neither can we or anyone else turn back the clock to give ourselves another chance.

We are free to choose, but, having chosen, we are not free to select the consequences of our choosing. We are, for example, free to drink a pint of whiskey, but, having done so, we are no longer free to be sober drivers. Our words and deeds have consequences — sometimes *tragic* consequences.

As we accept credit for our good choices, we also accept blame for our bad ones. To do so is exceedingly painful, but it is the only way to a new beginning.

Prayer: O Lord, we confess the failures of our unchangeable past. Have mercy on us. In Jesus' name. Amen

Thought for the day: "None is righteous, no, not one." (Romans 3:10)

"Grace Abounded All The More"

When overwhelmed with regret, we remember we are not alone. Moses was a murderer. David was guilty of both adultery and murder. With lies and curses, Peter denied his Lord. Paul consented to the stoning of Stephen. The Bible is realistic in presenting the sins of its heroes.

These are revealed not to minimize the significance of sin, but to maximize the mercy of God. Paul sums it up, "Where sin increased, grace abounded all the more." (Romans 5:20) Those words assure us that our sins are not too big for God to forgive. They are big enough, but God's love is bigger still! Pride tempts us to think that we have no sins, and it is also pride that tempts us to think that our sins are too big for God to forgive.

Take these words to heart: "If we confess our sins, [God] is faithful and just, and will forgive our sins and cleanse us from all unrighteousness." (1 John 1:9) This promise invites us to stop condemning ourselves and to start confessing our sins and trusting God's mercy.

Prayer: O Lord, thank you for your forgiveness in Jesus Christ. Thank you for loving us just as we are. In Jesus' name. Amen

Thought for the day: No sin is too big for God to forgive.

| Week Five | ***But I Still*** | Luke 15:11-24 |
| Day Five | ***Feel Guilty*** | 1 Timothy 1:12-17 |

Even when assured of God's forgiveness we often continue to feel guilty. The old sense of regret is still there. Memories of our tragic failure still haunt our days and nights. It is easy for us to interpret these feelings as a sign that we are not forgiven, but to do so is to misunderstand what forgiveness does and does not do.

In *Guilt and Grace*, Paul Tournier points out that forgiveness does not remove our feelings of guilt. When an action has been hurtful, we rightly regret it as long as we live. God's forgiveness does not make us feel grateful that it happened. The Apostle Paul was always ashamed to have been a party to Stephen's death and a persecutor of Christians. The prodigal son was welcomed home, but he still regretted his wasted life.

Forgiveness does not remove our feelings of regret, but it does restore us in the love of God. Forgiveness does not erase the past; it tells us that we are loved today and will be loved tomorrow. Whatever our feelings of regret, God assures us in Christ that he loves us now and will love us forever.

Prayer: Thank you, O Lord, that our faith rests not on our feelings, but on your promises. Keep us ever in the assurance of your love. In Jesus' name. Amen

Thought for the day: Whatever my feelings tell me, God in Christ says, "I love you, and will love you forever."

Grist For God's Mill

Even as we accept the regrettable aspects of the unchangeable past, we are open to the possibilities of the grace-filled present and future. Everything that happens is grist for God's mill. Our mistakes are bad, but God is able to use them for good.

Romans 8:28 can be translated: "Everything works for good with those who love God." What do we make of that? All things are not good in themselves and some work for evil, including with those who love God. Some, for example, have lost their faith through suffering. The Revised Standard Version's preferred translation of the same verse is, "In everything God works for good with those who love him." That's good news we dare to believe. Things may be bad, but God is still at work for good!

Our worst failures and most tragic mistakes certainly grieve God but they do not ultimately frustrate his life-giving will for us. God uses sin and suffering to turn us to his grace. God brings victory out of defeat and life out of death!

Prayer: We bow before your creative power, O Lord. Work to bring your good out of our evil. In Jesus' name. Amen

Thought for the day: When things are bad, God still works for good.

The Best Out   Job 42:10-17
Of The Worst   Acts 2:22-24
1 Corinthians 15:3-28

Some losses are restored in life. Job's lost fortunes were restored twofold. But it is not always so. Some illnesses are not healed; some live while others die.

Of all the miseries of life, is any greater than awareness of having contributed to our own or to another's suffering or death? When these feelings reflect the truth, where then is hope?

Our hope is in God, who continues to work for good *in everything*. We don't know why some are healed while others die. But in Christ we are promised the final healing of resurrection. When the doctor says, "I can do no more," God says, "Trust me, and see what I will do."

Jesus was "crucified and killed by the hands of lawless men. But God raised him up, having loosed the pangs of death, because it was not possible for him to be held by it." (Acts 2:23-24) E. Stanley Jones says that "God took the worst thing that ever happened, the crucifixion of Christ, and made it into the best thing that ever happened, the redemption of the world." This is our hope in life and death. Our worst failures are within the redemptive reach of God's creative love.

Prayer: Lord of life, turn our tragedies into your triumphs. Amen

Thought for the day: My worst is grist for God's best.

The Weight of Resentment

Our grief is often mingled with both regret and resentment. Some anger is justified. As it is right to be angry with ourselves over our failure, it is also proper to be angry with the hurtful behavior of others. As Jesus drove out the moneychangers, we too are freed to be angry against wrong.

We often hurt one another. Others suffer from our sins and we from theirs. None of us is perfect. Nor has anyone had a perfect parent, partner, relative, or friend. We all fail and hurt one another.

Failures have consequences: doctors make mistakes, drivers kill, we neglect our health, homes are broken by unfaithfulness. Such experiences as these may move us to intense resentment. Unless dealt with, this anger can act like a corrosive acid, poisoning our lives and our relationships.

Our anger needs to be faced and felt. With whom are we angry? How do we really feel? Is it justified? How can we express it constructively?

Prayer: O Lord, keep us honest with our feelings and give us wisdom to deal with them constructively. In Jesus' name. Amen

Thought for the day: I will face and feel my anger.

"Be Angry, But Sin Not"

The Bible advocates anger: "Be angry, but sin not." (Psalm 4:4) Another verse says, "Be angry but do not sin." (Ephesians 4:26) There is a proper as well as a sinful kind of anger. Sinful anger is hurtful; rightful anger is healthy and helpful.

Having said, "Be angry but do not sin," Paul goes on to urge, "Do not let the sun go down on your anger, and give no opportunity to the devil." (Ephesians 4:26, 27) We are not to harbor hostilities. When stored within, anger often grows into bitterness.

Anger needs to be confessed — not always as a sin, but always as a fact. When we do so, it is best to share our own feelings rather than attack another person. It is better to say, "I feel hurt and angry." It is not helpful to say, "You are mean and unkind." One is a confession, the other an accusation. The first is totally true; the second, at best, a partial truth. We are to speak "the truth in love" (Ephesians 4:15); and, when we express anger, are to do so with truth and love.

It is sometimes impossible or unwise to express anger to the one who offended us. That person may be dead or unable to understand. To say something may only make matters worse. Sharing such angry feelings with a pastor or trusted friend can prevent righteous indignation from growing into a sinful grudge.

Prayer: O Lord, free us to confess our feelings; stop us from attacking others. In Jesus' name. Amen

Thought for the day: Confessing helps; accusing hurts.

Forgive As Matthew 18:23-35
God Forgives Ephesians 4:29-32

After saying "Be angry but do not sin" (Ephesians 4:26), Paul goes on to say, "Let all bitterness and wrath and anger and clamor and slander be put away from you, with all malice, and be kind to one another, tenderhearted, forgiving one another, as God in Christ forgave you." (Ephesians 4:31-32) Having expressed our anger, we are to forgive as we are forgiven.

This is often beyond our ability. When we can't forgive, we should ponder Jesus' story of one who was forgiven much, yet forgave little. (See Matthew 18:23-35) The man in that story lacked the perspective and sense of humor to see his forgiving of another in the light of his own need of forgiveness. Seeing God's total forgiveness of our sins helps free us to forgive others.

As being forgiven does not remove all feelings of regret, so also forgiving others does not make us happy over what happened. Forgiving accepts the hurtful person but does not eliminate all hurt feelings. To forgive is to act with love, and to *love* is not always to *like*. To love is to act for the best and may even result in our saying, "Because we love and wish good for each other, it is best that we separate."

Prayer: Oh Lord, give us love to be kind, tenderhearted, and forgiving, as you are to us. In Jesus' name. Amen

Thought for the day: As God forgives me, I will forgive others.

Some anger is justified, but much is not. Many alcoholics, for example, rage against those who confront them with their illness but, when treatment is successful, those feelings often change to gratitude that confesses, "I could have killed you, but now I want to thank you for caring enough to confront me with my illness and get me into treatment."

A loss may also confront us with unpleasant facts about ourselves, facts that make us angry. Have we depended on another person to do things we should have done for ourselves? Did we even make a "god" of someone on whom we relied too much? Have we been living mainly to fulfil a role of husband, wife, parent, child or employee rather than as a person in our own right? Are we now, like the confronted alcoholic, angry because our wrongful living has been revealed to us?

The truth hurts — especially when accompanied by the pain of loss and loneliness. Paul asked the Galatians, "Have I then become your enemy by telling you the truth?" (Galatians 4:16) We also ask ourselves, "Have I been wronged, or am I resentful for being confronted with the truth?" When the latter is true, we need courage to face that truth and admit our fault.

Prayer: O Lord, save us from sinful anger. Forgive and heal us. In Jesus' name. Amen

Thought for the day: Truth is not my enemy but my friend.

Is death our friend? Are we to bow obediently when the grim reaper calls and accept death as being for the best? Some say so, but the New Testament does not. The Apostle Paul speaks of death as "the last enemy." (1 Corinthians 15:26) Jesus opposed sickness and death. He healed the sick, raised the dead, and proclaimed that he had come that we might "have life, and have it abundantly." (John 10:10) Death itself is doomed to die: "Then Death and Hades were thrown into the lake of fire. This is the second death." (Revelation 20:14)

Therefore, when tragic death strikes down a life filled with hope and promise, it is right to be angry. We need not suppress our resentment as if that were the only Christian thing to do. With Dylan Thomas we rightly "rage, rage against the dying of the light." That rage affirms our faith that God is on the side of life.

When death comes as a blessing, it is not because death is good but because life has become so bad. If death is a blessing, real life has already died. All that destroys life is not our friend but our enemy.

Prayer: O Lord, save us from affirming what you deny and denying what you affirm. Keep us solidly on the side of life. Amen

Thought for the day: Rejoicing in life, we rightly rage against death.

In times of grief, the whole world may seem hostile and forboding. Evil has triumphed; goodness seems gone. We have not only lost a loved one; we have lost a friendly world. With Paul we feel that "we are not contending against flesh and blood, but against the principalities, against the powers, against the world rulers of this present darkness, against the spiritual hosts of wickedness in the heavenly places." (Ephesians 6:12) When this happens we are not to submit to evil, but are to fight these "hosts of wickedness," armed with "the whole armor of God." (Ephesians 6:11)

Jesus fought the powers of darkness and taught us to pray, "Deliver us from evil." (Matthew 6:13) John states, "The reason the Son of God appeared was to destroy the works of the devil." (1 John 3:8) We may wonder if there is a personal devil, but when the universe seems set against us, we have no doubt that demonic powers are at work in the world. Since Christ came to destroy those forces, it is right for us to rage and work against them all.

Prayer: Lord, save us from thinking that we are to submit to evil. Deliver us from evil and give us courage to work for all that is good. In Jesus' name. Amen

Thought for the day: When Evil rages, we too should rage.

"Out Of The Depths I Cry"

When overwhelmed by grief, we may not only feel that we have lost a friendly world, but also that we have lost a friendly God. Can we love a God who creates a world like this? How can we keep faith in a God of love in the face of such suffering? As we rage against evil, must we not also rage against God, who lets it happen? And is it right to rage against God?

Whether right or not, there is no sense in playing make-believe with God. We are to worship God "in spirit and truth" (John 3:24), and are surely to be honest in telling God the anguish and anger we feel. As Jesus cried, "My God, my God, why hast thou forsaken me?" (Matthew 27:46), we too pour out our pain in prayer, confident that God can take it all. Like frustrated children kicking the shins of a parent whose ways seem cruel and contradictory, we too can strike out at God, confident that he understands and loves.

It may even be that the real object of our rage is not God but Satan. At any rate, Krister Stendahl is right — when tragedy strikes, it often helps to believe in the devil.

Prayer: Out of the depths we cry to you, O God. Lead us out of this darkness into light. In Jesus' name. Amen

Thought for the day: It is safe to be honest with God.

Week Seven   Lamentations 3:33
Day One   *The Will of God* Matthew 18:14
               Ephesians 1:3-12

Tragic events are often labeled "the will of God" or even "acts of God." But are they so? A drunk kills a child. Is drunken driving the will of God? Doctors fail to save a life. Was the accident or illness the will of God, and, if so, were the doctors opposing God? Deaths from smallpox and polio were once common and often said to be God's will. Did those who developed vaccines that spare us these illnesses rebel against God? Are we who use them acting against God's will? When Jesus sent disciples to heal disease and infirmity (Matthew 10:1), did they oppose God?

From such examples, it is clear that sin and sickness are not God's will for us. God permits but does not desire sin. God permits sickness, suffering, and death; but if he is like Jesus, God does not desire these things for us. He wills and works only for good. This does not explain why God permits what he does not desire, but it does keep us from thinking tragedy is sent from God.

Prayer: O Lord, keep us in confidence that your will is for good and against evil. Strengthen us to work with you for a better world. In Jesus' name. Amen

Thought for the day: God gets the credit; evil gets the blame.

There is comfort in regarding terrible events as deeds of a God of love. This view sees tragedy as goodness in disguise. We can then say, "It seemed bad, but since God did it, it must be good."

This is a comforting thought, but is it true? If so, there is really no evil but only the appearance of evil. This is not the view of reality we receive from Jesus. When he taught us to pray for deliverance from evil, he meant business. To Jesus, evil was a reality with which we have to deal. Sin, sickness, and death are not illusions but enemies.

It is, of course, possible to believe the good to be bad and the bad to be good. We may, for example, hate the medicine and exercise that can save our lives and love the cigarettes and excessive food that can kill us. Much that is "exalted among men is an abomination in the sight of God" (Luke 16:15), and what we despise may look good to God. We may confuse good and bad, but let there be no confusion on this: evil is real — it is not just goodness in disguise.

Prayer: O Lord, save us from the false comforts of make-believe. Thank you for Jesus' revelation of reality. In his name. Amen

Thought for the day: I want comfort, but not the false comfort of make-believe.

Week Seven   *"In Everything*   Gen. 45:8; 50:15-21
Day Three   *God Works*   Romans 8:28
                 For Good"   2 Cor. 12:7-9

Our comfort in terrible times is not in pretending that evil is good, but in trusting the goodness of God. To see this comfort, we contrast the perspectives of Joseph and Paul. Joseph told his brothers who had sold him into slavery: "Do not be distressed, or angry with yourselves, because you sold me here; for God sent me before you to preserve life . . . You meant evil against me; but God meant it for good." (Genesis 45:5 and 50:20) Here Joseph expresses an evil-is-goodness-in-disguise point of view.

Paul says, "*In everything* God works for good with those who love him." (Romans 8:28; my emphasis) It is not things that are good, but God who works for good in them. Paul illustrates his point of view by telling of his "thorn in the flesh." He calls this affliction "a messenger of Satan" and prays to be rid of it. Yet he thanks God for using this evil to reveal that "my grace is sufficient for you." (2 Corinthians 12:7-9) This is our best comfort — that in everything, good and bad, God works for good. He uses sin to lead us into his mercy, illness to bring us to trust his strength, death to usher us into new life; but we do not thank God for sin, sickness, or death — we thank God for God.

Prayer: O God, comfort us now with the assurance of your love and the creative possibilities of your might. In Jesus' name. Amen

Thought for the day: Bad is bad, but God works for good.

God Has the Acts 2:22-24
Next Move 1 Thessalonians 4:13-18

God took the sin of Joseph's brothers and used it to prevent starvation. Through Paul's thorn in the flesh he revealed his grace. God transformed the sinful crucifixion of Christ into the redemption of the world and used Jesus' death to demonstrate his power to give new life.

Our hope is not that those who betrayed and murdered Jesus were really doing good things. He was "crucified and killed by the hands of lawless men." (Acts 2:23) These were sins for which Jesus prayed that they be forgiven. (Luke 23:24) Our hope is not in the disguised goodness of sinners, but in the revealed goodness of God, who, through the sufferings, death, and resurrection of Christ, exposes his heart of love and saving power. Looking to Christ, we dare believe that God is not defeated by evil. All may look hopeless to us, but it is not so to him. God always has the next move. Life's tragedies do not checkmate the Almighty.

Have dreams of life together died in the dust of death, divorce, or broken love? Then Christ says, in effect, "Grieve, but not as those who have no hope; trust me to give hope to your broken hearts."

Prayer: O Lord, we grieve and yet we dare to hope. Keep us in this trust. In Jesus' name. Amen

Thought for the day: There is no checkmate for God.

God's Will
and Our Destiny

When thinking of God's will, we distinguish between what God desires and what he permits. Today we ask, What does God desire for us? The New Testament affirms a destiny of life in love.

Jesus said, "It is not the will of my Father who is in heaven that one of these little ones should perish." (Matthew 18:14)

Paul declares, "Blessed be the God and Father of our Lord Jesus Christ . . . He destined us in love to be his sons through Jesus Christ, according to the purpose of his will . . . In him, . . . we who first hoped in Christ have been destined and appointed to live for the praise of his glory." (Ephesians 1:3, 5, 11-12)

"God has not destined us for wrath, but to obtain salvation through our Lord Jesus Christ." (1 Thessalonians 5:9)

"This is good, and it is acceptable in the sight of God our Savior, who desires all men to be saved and to come to the knowledge of truth." (1 Timothy 2:3)

God wills us all to live in his love and to share his salvation. When we pray, "Thy will be done," we are asking God to fulfil in us this destiny of love. We may fear this prayer, thinking that then dreadful things will happen. Loving as God wills can lead to a cross; but even so, "Thy will be done" is still our safest prayer.

Prayer: O Lord, fulfil in us, and in all, your destiny of life in love. In Jesus' name. Amen

Thought for the day: God's great desire is our greatest good.

In times of loss, we may feel doomed for death rather than destined for life. When our failures seem fatal and the future looks hopeless, when we gaze into a cold starry sky or stand in a teeming crowd and wonder if we matter to anyone, when our hopes and dreams come crashing down about us, then it is hard to believe that we are destined for anything beyond disappointment and despair.

Christian realism compels us to confront evil and to face our faults and finitude. Honesty admits some stories end sadly. But Christian realism also invites us to see Jesus as the daystar of our destiny. We need not look only to sickness, sorrow, and death. Instead of that we can focus on Jesus. Whatever our troubles, we are to "run with perseverance the race that is set before us, looking to Jesus the pioneer and perfector of our faith, who for the joy that was set before him endured the cross, despising the shame, and is seated at the right hand of the throne of God." By centering on Jesus "who endured from sinners, such hostility against himself," we are kept from growing "weary or fainthearted." (Hebrews 12:1-3)

Prayer: O Lord, give us courage to face the harsh realities, but even more, give us eyes of faith to see Jesus. In his name. Amen

Thought for the day: Through troubled times we look to Jesus and take help and hope from him.

In Christ we yield to God but resist all evil. When we wrongly see evil as sent from God, we must either yield to evil or rebel against God as we resist it. But when we see God opposing evil, we are enabled to yield to God and at the same time dedicate ourselves to work for the elimination of all sickness and suffering, assured that we work with God's blessing. Surrendered to God, we are rebels with Jesus, committed to battle the foes of life and to affirm all that enables, enhances and ennobles life.

We don't know why we live in an imperfect world, but it is clear in Christ that we are to do all we can to make it better. We are living in what has been called "the eighth day of creation" and are to be creatively at work with God to help bring it to completion.

In all life-giving work, we trust God's blessing; and when life is done, we entrust our loved ones and ourselves to Jesus' promise: "This is the will of my Father, that every one who sees the Son and believes in him should have eternal life; and I will raise him up at the last day." (John 6:40)

Prayer: Spirit of God, by your grace fulfil in us your will to give us life. In Jesus' name. Amen

Thought for the day: My will to live echoes God's will to give me life in fulness.

When tragedy strikes we wonder: Why? Why to him? Why to her? Why to me? This *Why?* asks two questions: From what cause? and For what purpose?

When we ask, "From what cause?" one answer often raises another question, until we must say, "I don't know." "Why did he die?" "From cancer." "Why from cancer?" "Cancer is in the world." "Why is cancer in the world?" "I don't know."

There are at least three sources of our suffering: it can come from 1. ourselves; 2. other people; and 3. factors seemingly unrelated to human failure.

If we kill ourselves by smoking, it's our fault. If someone else kills us, it's their fault. But if, after having done all we could for good health, we still get cancer, whose fault is that? Perhaps it is the fault of the human race! Had humanity worked as hard to destroy cancer as to get rich, reach the moon, or build bombs, cancer might have been already conquered.

But we still ask, "Why does God permit cancer in his world?" We don't know, but the healing ministry of Jesus assures us that sickness is not God's will for us and that we are to work to rid the world of illness.

Prayer: O Lord, give light for each day's journey and love through each dark night. In Jesus' name. Amen

Thought for the day: We sometimes wonder why, and often find that none can answer.

Week Eight   John 9:1-7
Day Two   *Acts of God?*

Jesus did not attribute all suffering to human failure, nor did he see it as sent from God. When asked, "Who sinned, this man or his parents, that he was born blind?" Jesus answered, "It was not that this man sinned, or his parents, but that the works of God might be manifest in him." (John 9:2-3) This reply gives no explanation of the birth defect, but it does reject blaming it on either human sin or divine intention. For Jesus it was an occasion to show that real acts of God are works of healing. Here we see that life-giving deeds are true "acts of God" and not the unexplainable tragedies that are often labeled as such. When a tornado kills a family let's not call it "an act of God" and blame him for it. But, when a tornado warning system and storm shelters save a community from injury, let's say, "Thanks be to God!"

Such considerations do not explain everything. Sunshine and storm, sickness and health come to good and bad alike. This is a hazardous, as well as beautiful world in which to live. When we are blessed, it is not a sign of special favor — nor, when we suffer, of special punishment. Such is the way of the world. As we strive to make it better, Jesus assures us that we are doing the works of God.

Prayer: Thank you, Lord, for working still. Give us love to do your works. In Jesus' name. Amen

Thought for the day: Only Christ-like deeds are acts of God.

60

"Why?" also asks, For what purpose did this happen? What lesson is God trying to teach? These questions see all events as deeds of God. But when a drunk kills a child, is it right to ask, "Why did God do it?" God *didn't* do it! Even when death results from disease, we don't say, "God did it." When healing comes we say, "Thanks be to God." When disease triumphs we do not blame God, but trust him still to answer our prayers in the final healing of resurrection.

Everything that happens is not for some good purpose. Some events are as senseless as we feel them to be. Does this rob us of comfort? No. It leads to true comfort in the love and power of God, who bears the anguish of senseless suffering and has power to triumph over every evil.

This perspective also frees us from an implied judgment. If a tragedy is sent to "teach me something'" it's really my fault. If I didn't need this lesson, God would not have to teach it. God certainly teaches lessons in times of trouble, but that does not mean that he sends suffering for that purpose. God does no evil, but God does use evil for good.

Prayer: O Lord, by your creative power, bring some good out of the senseless suffering of our lives. In Jesus' name. Amen

Thought for the day: No evil is sent from God but God uses evil to reveal his good.

Job 5:1-7
It's Not Fair!   Matthew 5:43-48

It is easy to feel that we have done something to deserve both our blessings and our sufferings. Joys seem a reward; miseries a punishment. But life is not so fair. It is difficult to live with the fact that some joys and some sorrows come to good and bad alike, but that's the way it is.

We receive blessings beyond our deserving. If we ask, "What did I do to deserve this pain?", we should also ask, "What did I do to deserve this joy?" Our greatest blessings are unmerited gifts of God's grace and people's love.

Much suffering is also undeserved. Deeds have consequences. "A man reaps what he sows." (Galatians 6:7, NEB) But we also reap what we never sowed. As our pride needs reminding that we don't deserve all blessing, our egos need assurance we don't merit all misery. If sickness were the just due of those who suffer, Jesus would have been unjust in his healing ministry, and his own suffering would have been a sure sign of his own sinfulness.

Prayer: Thank you, Lord, for blessings beyond deserving. Give us courage to endure unmerited suffering and compassion to care for others who suffer unjustly. In Jesus' name. Amen

Thought for the day: We often fare far better than we deserve.

2 Samuel 18:31-33
Why Not Me?

In loss and loneliness we often ask, "Why did this happen to me?" and feel our sufferings to be unfair. But isn't it equally unfair when others suffer while do we not? We sometimes act as if there is nothing wrong when *others* suffer, but that it is a great injustice for anything bad to happen to *us*.

It is selfish to ignore the suffering of others while considering it unfair that trouble comes to us. After an assault of personal pain, we may even say, "Now I can't believe in God anymore." But what enabled us to believe in God while others were suffering all around us? If suffering destroys faith, we need not wait until we feel it in ourselves.

But we are not altogether selfish. We also ask, "Why am I alive and healthy while others are sick and dying?" Such questions need not lead to the self-righteous arrogance that assumes that we suffer less because we are better than others. They can rather move us to profound gratitude for gifts beyond our deserving and to a deeper compassion for those, no less righteous than ourselves, whose sufferings are far greater than our own.

Prayer: O Lord, help us be more forgetful of ourselves and more caring for others. In Jesus' name. Amen

Thought for the day: When I ask, "Why me?" I must also ask "Why not me?"

When someone asks, "Why did he die?", another may answer, "His time was up!" There is some comfort in this kind of thinking. It assumes that God has a plan for each of our lives and that we live until our allotted time runs out. Someone who thinks this way believes that a person killed in an accident would, in any case, have died from something else and that when our number comes up God takes us and there is nothing we can do about it.

The perspective of Scripture does not support such thinking. From the Bible, as well as from personal experience, we see that we are not marionettes dangling from God's hand. As Christians, we do not believe that we are preordained to a certain length of life. Our freedom enables choices that affect our dying as well as our living. We are stewards of life and are commissioned by Christ to care for our health, for the health of others and even for the present and future health and welfare of the entire planet. By doing so, we can add years to life and life to years.

Prayer: Thank you, Lord, for the blessing of life. Help us to be better stewards of our lives and of the life of the world. In Jesus' name. Amen

Thought for the day: Our deeds affect our years and the years of others.

Better Than Explanation

Jesus did not explain everything. He did not tell why a man was born blind, why some are healthy while others are sick, why some live when others die. We live with mystery and confess with Paul, "Now we see in a mirror dimly." (1 Corinthians 13:12a) In this darkness, Paul invites us to trust that one day we shall "understand fully, even as [we] have been fully understood." (1 Corinthians 13:12b)

In the meantime, our confidence is sustained by Jesus' promise: "In the world you will have trouble. But courage! The victory is mine; I have conquered the world." (John 16:33, NEB) Whatever has happened or will happen, this is still "our Father's world," and "though the wrong seems oft so strong, God is the ruler yet."

God's promises don't explain our troubles, but they can transform our lives. When crushed by grief, we need more than an explanation. We need love and power to renew our strength and give us faith and hope. God's promises in Christ offer that transformation. He promises to bring us through to victory.

Prayer: O Lord, thank you for your transforming power. Save us from being conformed to the cynicism of the world. Keep on transforming us day by day toward the likeness of Christ. In his name we pray. Amen

Thought for the day: Jesus explains much and transforms more.

Our Quest
for Meaning

Loss of a loved one makes us wonder what life means and sometimes to question the worth of going on. F. W. Robertson states our feeling and our task: "We are here to live and die; in a few years it will all be over; meanwhile, what we have to do is try to understand, and to help one another to understand, what it all means — what this strange and contradictory thing, which we call life, contains within it."

Troubled times tempt us to take our mood from the seemingly senseless circumstances. But this is like taking our bearings from a compass that is being thrown off by its environment. When the compass points one way and the North Star stands in another, wise explorers take their bearings from the star.

Our inner compass is often thrown off by traumatic experiences. We therefore look to Jesus and take our bearings from him. Our thoughts and feelings can lead us astray; Christ leads us back to God and to ourselves. "As it is, we do not yet see everything in subjection to him. But we see Jesus . . ." (Hebrews 2:8-9)

Prayer: Spirit of Christ, we look to you. Be the sun of all our days and the guiding star of every night. Amen

Thought for the day: Christ is our compass; we look to him to guide us.

Week Nine　　　*On Doubting*　　　John 20:24-31
Day Two　　　　*Our Doubts*

We sometimes sense God's presence with such close-ness that he seems more real than ever before. These ex-periences confirm the promises of Christ and give a serenity we had believed impossible in the midst of sorrow.

On other occasions, God seems gone and we don't know what we believe. We may wonder if there is a God, and doubt that life has meaning. Harry Emerson Fosdick believed that those who dared question cherished false-hoods are among the heroes of history. But he also urged us to "doubt our doubts" and suggested that we set our doubts alongside the convictions of Jesus and ask, "Who is likely correct — me in my doubts, or Jesus in his faith?"

Is our present, grief-shaped view of a cold and god-less world more likely correct than Jesus' confidence in the warmth of his Father's love? Can we really doubt the right-ness of the love we see in Jesus? Could he be so right in his love and yet so wrong in his faith? In light of the confi-dence and convictions of Jesus we rightly "doubt our doubts" and turn again to trust God's love.

Prayer: O God, in Jesus we see love and faith that call us again to trust your love. Thank you. Amen

Thought for the day: Our doubts and fears fade beside Jesus' faith.

Day Three   *Believe What You Can*

A friend, when filled with doubt, was told by an understanding pastor, "Believe what you can." Those wise words remind us that the Christian Gospel is not a required idea that we must believe in order to get God to love us. We are not saved by believing good thoughts any more than by doing good works, and we need beware lest we try to save ourselves by holding a correct theology.

The Gospel is the declaration not of a theology to be believed, but of a promise to be trusted. Christ assures us that God loves us in our doubt as well as in our sin. Grace welcomes us just as we are, doubts and all.

As one example of what this means for us, remember that heaven is not promised only to those who have no doubt of the Resurrection, but to all who rest their lives in the grace of God. The Easter message is not just to convince us that something happened then, but to call us to trust in God who promises to lift us now to newness of life and then, beyond our dying, to raise us again to fullness of life in heaven.

> **Prayer:**   Just as I am, though tossed about
> With many a conflict, many a doubt,
> Fightings and fears within, without.
> O Lamb of God, I come, I come. Amen.

Thought for the day: God loves doubters as well as sinners.

Week Nine
Day Four

By Grace
Through Faith

Ephesians 2:8-10
Romans 10:14-17

We are not saved *because of or on account of* our faith. Our hope is in neither our good faith nor our good works, but in the goodness of God. Paul says, "For by grace you have been saved through faith; and this is not your own doing, it is the gift of God — not because of works, lest any man should boast." (Ephesians 2:8, 9)

Salvation is "*by* grace . . . *through* faith." God saves us. Faith permits, but does not cause, our salvation: having faith is being actively passive to God's action. It is "letting go and letting God."

We do not create faith by trying to have it. "Faith comes from what is heard and what is heard comes by the preaching of Christ." (Romans 10:17) Faith is born in our hearts as we hear the promises of God's love. It is all, as Paul Scherer liked to say, more akin to courtship than the courtroom. In Christ, God woos us to trust him.

When we try to trust, we are still seeking to do something to save ourselves. When we quit trying and look to God's promises in Christ, we begin trusting. Resting in these promises, we let God do the saving God alone can do.

Prayer: God of grace, woo us again to live by your mercy and might. In Jesus' name. Amen

Thought for the day: God doesn't help us save ourselves. God saves us without our help.

Alvin Rogness likes to say that "the worst thing about being an atheist is having no one to thank." When life is terrible, it is possible to stoically endure it. But when we are overwhelmed by joy and overflowing with gratitude, what can we do with no one to thank?

It is difficult to reconcile the goodness of God with the world's evil; but, for many of us, it is impossible to reconcile the goodness of the world with the absence of a good God. Our intellectual problems are not solved by dismissing a God of love from the universe. We then face "the problem of goodness" — how do we explain the beauty, joy, and meaning that are also a part of life?

Even now, we see the miracle of our own lives, shattered as they may be, and recall the joyful moments of love we have known. We ponder the beauty of sunsets and symphonies, flowers and friendships. Above all, we think of Jesus, who came through sin and suffering to become our beautiful Savior. Remembering all this, we again dare believe that there is someone to thank.

Prayer: Thank you, God, for being with us to receive our thanks. We give you praise for all things good. In Jesus' name. Amen

Thought for the day: Today we ponder all things good and beautiful and are moved to praise and thanksgiving.

Venture on John 1:43-51
God's Promises John 14:1-11

E. Stanley Jones said, "If the Christian faith is not true, it ought to be true." If it is untrue, the lies presented by Jesus are a strange kind of falsehood. They make sense of life and are creative of the highest virtues we know. If Jesus' truth were an illusion, it would be better for us to live with despair than with hope, with contempt rather than compassion. But we simply cannot live well that way. We live better by Jesus' "lies" than by any contrary "truth."

What would happen if everyone were to live with the faith and compassion of Christ? Would it not be a far better world? And what if all treated Christlikeness with contempt and tried to live contrary to all we learn from Jesus? It would be hell on earth! Can we then do better than take our chances with Jesus, trusting the realities revealed in him to be the bedrock of the universe?

Even when uncertain, we can begin to venture on Jesus' promises — living as if God loves us, trusting as if grace abounds for us, caring as if our deeds did count for something. When we do so, a voice within says, "This is it! This is authentic living! This is being the person I was born to be! This is living as I was designed to live!"

Prayer: Thank you, Lord, for the realities revealed in Jesus. We risk our all to live by them. In his name. Amen

Thought for the day: When I trust in Jesus he turns out to be true.

An Adventure of Abandonment

Among the most difficult, yet vital, lessons of life is this: "Whoever would save his life will lose it; and whoever loses his life for my sake, he will save it." (Luke 9:24-25) Here Jesus states two ways of life — one self-saving, the other self-losing. The first is self-defeating, the second self-fulfilling.

The self-saving way is a clinging, hanging-on style of life. It seeks to possess things, people, and ourselves. Self-preoccupation, self-centeredness and self-seeking are signs of its presence.

When we live this way, we are like a child so possessive of a pet rabbit that he clutches it to himself until it is squeezed to death. His eagerness to keep it kills it. So, too, with life: when we try to keep it as our private possession, life dies on our hands. But when we let life be lost in an adventure of abandonment — giving ourselves away in trust to God and with love to people — we begin to discover what it is to be alive.

Jesus' words are not true just because he said them. He said them because they are true. They witness to this fact of life: we are created to live an adventure of abandonment!

Prayer: O Lord, lured by your love, we give ourselves away. We surrender to you, forget ourselves, care for others and begin to live. In Jesus' name. Amen

Thought for the day: Saving life, we die; losing life, we live.

Coping With Every Matthew 28:16-20
Day

God in Christ invites us to let ourselves be loved and lifted. Jesus says, "Come to me, all who labor and who are heavy laden, and I will give you rest." (Matthew 11:28) Whatever happens, we are to rest in the love of God. But this same Jesus who says "Come to me" also says, "Go" for me. (Matthew 28:19) We are sent to love, witness, serve, and share. "As the Father has sent me, even so I send you." (John 20:21)

We sometimes feel compelled by the great commission to eagerly work and witness. But in grief we may feel like doing nothing. It may even seem that we can't do anything and that, if we could, it wouldn't be worth doing anyway.

If children or others are in our care, we realize that they also grieve and need our affection, but we are often too tired and irritable to be tender. To be told to care with Christlike love may seem far beyond us. When we are hardly getting through the day, how can we do more? When unable in ourselves, we need the enabling presence of Christ.

Prayer: O Lord, if we are to live with tender love, it must be by your power. Enable us now. In Jesus' name. Amen

Thought for the day: Strength to cope comes from Christ.

Week Ten   Galatians 5:22
Day Two   *Love And Self-Control*   2 Peter 1:2-11
                                            2 Timothy 1:7

In grief we struggle for self-control. Fearing collapse, we try to keep control and carry on. Although limited, each of us has some power of self-control. We can do things we don't want to do, and can even have some influence over what occupies our minds. Following a loss, we may seem to think only of the one who is absent and to relive the painful memories. But as time goes on, we can begin to turn our thoughts to other things. Having to do specific work that compels our attention is often a blessing. A hobby or volunteer activity can also help save us from wallowing in morbid thoughts and self-preoccupation.

Christ commands us to love, and we are urged to practice self-control: "Make every effort to supplement your faith . . . with self-control." (2 Peter 1:5-6) But both love and self-control are promised as well as commanded: "God did not give us a spirit of timidity but a spirit of power and love and self-control." (2 Timothy 1:7) Paul's list of "the fruit of the spirit" (Galatians 5:22) begins with love and ends with self-control. So, even as we try to love and keep self-control, we trust God to give us these good gifts and open our lives to receive them.

Prayer: By the power of your Spirit, increase in us your gifts of love and self-control. In Jesus' name. Amen

Thought for the day: When I am unable, God will enable.

An Open Secret

"I have learned the secret," says the Apostle Paul, "of facing plenty and hunger, abundance and want. I can do all things in him who strengthens me." (Philippians 4:12-13) Paul was acquainted with suffering and well aware of his inability to cope with adversity. But by the grace of God, he was given the confidence that no problems were too big for him and Christ to tackle together. In Christ, Paul was enabled to meet the best and the worst of life.

When Paul says he can do "all things," he does not mean flying to the moon or taking over for God, but doing "all things" Christ wanted him to do. In Christ, God invites our confidence that we will be enabled for everything that he wants us to do. We have limited talents, but each of us is given enough ability and enough grace to do what God wills. He does not expect us to be supermen or wonderwomen, but he does want us to complete the tasks at hand, sustained by the strength that Christ supplies. In this confidence we return to the duties of life.

Prayer: O Lord, save us from expecting more of ourselves than you do; forgive us for trying to do by our strength what we can do only by your power. Enable us to do this day's work today. In Jesus' name. Amen

Thought for the day: "I have strength for anything through him who gives me power." (Philippians 4:13, NEB)

Having confessed confidence in Christ, Paul goes on immediately to tell of help received from people: "I have strength for anything through him who gives me power. But it was kind of you to share the burden of my troubles." (Philippians 4:13-14, NEB) Paul was not ashamed of his dependence on God, nor was he too proud to receive help from people.

There is a sense in which no one can do our work for us, but others can help us do it. When broken with grief, we may be tempted to live as if on a desert island. We may be too proud to ask assistance from others or so humble that we hate to bother anyone to help us.

But Paul says, "Bear one another's burdens, and so fulfil the law of Christ." (Galatians 6:2) When we let others help, us they "fulfill the law of Christ," and who are we to hinder anyone from doing that? Paul is aware of the fact that there are burdens no one can lift from us: "Each [one] will have to bear his own load." (Galatians 6:5) But Paul also encourages us to welcome the help that others can give.

Prayer: O Lord, give us strength to bear our own load and wisdom to let others help along the way. In Jesus' name. Amen

Thought for the day: In times of loss all of us need all the help we can get.

Who Needs Me Now?

Our "most important people" include those we need
the most. Thank God for them! But there are also some
equally important people who need us. When bereaved,
we often doubt this and wonder, Who needs me now?

Because the loss of a loved one often comes at the
time of retirement, when we may also be feeling limita-
tions from aging, it can be difficult to maintain our sense
of usefulness. But of this we can be sure — there is someone who needs us. It is vital for us to seek and serve that
person. He or she may be one of our family or friends,
or someone else, far away, who can be blessed through
our service in church or community.

Inability to do everything we once did need not keep
us from something we can do now. Who knows the most
important deed in any life? Is it a "great" achievement of
long ago or a "small" kindness we do today? Jesus spoke
of a "cup of water" given in his name. (Mark 9:41) When
our physical abilities are limited we are still commanded
to "pray constantly." (1 Thessalonians 5:17) A vocation
of such prayerfulness may be the most significant work we
ever do.

Prayer: O God, give us eyes of love to see those
who need us, and enable us to serve, share, and pray to
bless their lives. In Jesus' name. Amen

Thought for the day: I can't do *everything*, but
I can do *something*, and I will do it today!

Called to Be Comforters

Paul speaks of the "God of all comfort, who comforts us in all our affliction, so that we may be able to comfort those who are in any affliction, with the comfort with which we ourselves are comforted by God." (2 Corinthians 1:3, 4) Those who understand grief, and know the comfort God provides, can be much help to others similarly bereaved. This does not mean rushing into someone's life with "I know exactly how you feel and this is what you are to do!" Since we don't wish to be treated in such an arrogant and coercive way, we will wisely refrain from imposing ourselves on others but we will make ourselves available to listen and to share.

Job's comforters helped most when they kept silence, "and no one spoke a word to him, for they saw that his suffering was very great." (Job 2:13) We may help most by just being there, available as needed. Some comments are, of course, in order. A quiet confession of our own experience and a simple witness to promises that have sustained us can give supportive assurance.

Many congregations have "Friendly Visitor" programs that provide regular contact and conversation with shut-ins and the bereaved. If there is such a group in your church, join it; if not, explore the possibilities of starting one.

Prayer: O God of all comfort, help us to share ourselves and your presence with others. In Jesus' name. Amen

Thought for the day: God's comfort is ours to share.

                                    1 Corinthians 15:58

Day Seven   ***Deeds That Count***   Matthew 25:31-40

When we wonder if our work and our prayers count for anything, it is well to recall a commission from Paul. Having proclaimed the Resurrection, he says, "Therefore, my beloved brethren, be steadfast, immovable, always abounding in the work of the Lord, knowing that in the Lord your labor is not in vain." (1 Corinthians 15:58)

We have noted the fact that the most significant deed of our lives may be a "little" act of kindness that is soon forgotten. After some deed of love we, like those in Jesus' parable, may be surprised to hear, "As you did it to one of the least of these my brethren, you did it to me." (Matthew 25:40)

Now Paul reminds us that our deeds have an eternal significance. "In the Lord [our] labor is not in vain." Every good work, however unnoticed, is a vital event within the sweep of time and eternity. It may even affect the temporal or eternal salvation of some other person!

Harry Emerson Fosdick liked to say that "we need not be great in ourselves to stand for something great." Neither do we need to be great to be used by a great God who wills to use our deeds and prayers as means of temporal and eternal blessing. "Therefore" we keep working and praying in confidence that our "labor is not in vain."

Prayer: O Lord, keep us steadfast in works of love; show us what to do and give us strength to do it today. Amen

Thought for the day: Love's labor is never lost.

Decision Making

After years of deciding things together, it is often difficult to make decisions alone. We can no longer tell a salesperson, "I will have to talk this over with my husband, or wife." Now the responsibility for decision making is ours alone.

We may have left many matters almost entirely to our spouse and may now discover that we know next to nothing about paying bills, repairing the car, or shopping for gifts or groceries. Having full responsibility for child care and money management may be a new and frightening experience. Beyond such daily concerns, there may be larger decisions to be made. "Should I stay here and keep the house or move to an apartment?" "Would it be best for me to go to work?" There are no easy answers to such questions. Take time to deal with each one and seek counsel from a wise friend or family member.

Taking time and seeking counsel can help avoid impulsive decisions that add to our grief. We have lost enough and need beware of choices that lead to regret. Thoughtfulness now will be ground for future gratitude.

Prayer: O Lord, give us wisdom to choose rightly in matters large and small. Grant guidance for the details of the day and the choices of a lifetime. In Jesus' name. Amen

Thought for the day: I will take time and seek wisdom to make right choices.

In times of grief, indecision is often the best decision. We may, for example, be tempted to quickly sell the house and move to an apartment or new community. This may be wise but it is well to ponder carefully before doing so. We may fear living alone, and the lonely house may abound with reminders that prompt our tears. But leaving may only add to our grief. Loss of place would be added to loss of a person. Therefore, it is often well to stay put at least for awhile.

There are exceptions to this rule. If new to a community where we have neither place nor people, it may be wise to relocate near friends and family. It may be impossible to live alone and necessary to live with someone or move to a retirement center. But it is usually best to keep disruption to a minimum.

Loss of familiar places causes grief similar to the loss of a person. Children need to understand that a move from home to nursing home can plunge a parent into mourning. The move may be essential, but the loss of home is still grounds for grief to be met with understanding. Wise compassion limits losses and postpones disruption to give time to work through the initial shock and anguish of grief.

Prayer: O Lord, teach us when to act and when to wait. Save us from impulsive actions we will later regret and from fear that keeps us from doing what must be done now. In Jesus' name. Amen

Thought for the day: When grieving I will seek to avoid choices that lead to greater loss and greater grief.

Promises to Be Broken

Among our most difficult decisions are those related to promises made before the death or separation occurred. We may have consented to deathbed requests that we couldn't or shouldn't carry out. Perhaps we agreed to live with our spouse's family or to never marry again. Now we feel guilty and perplexed. Do we sin and betray our love by going back on such promises?

While promises should never be broken lightly, there are times to break them. When accused of breaking certain promises, Abraham Lincoln replied that promises he should never have made in the first place were better off broken than kept. There is wisdom and freedom in his example. If it was a mistake to make a promise, it is likely a mistake to keep it. Promises made in the tension of terminal illness and vows declared in the heat of separation are often mistaken.

Jephthah vowed that if successful in battle, he would sacrifice the first person who came out to meet him on his return home. When met by his only child after a victorious battle, Jephthah was grief-stricken; yet he believed he could not go back on his promise and the account says, "Her father . . . did with her according to his vow which he had made." (Judges 11:39) We cannot imagine Jesus blessing such a vow or requiring that it be fulfilled. Such promises should never bind us.

Prayer: O Lord, save us from making foolish promises. Enable us to keep good promises and give us courage to break the bad ones. In Jesus' name. Amen

Thought for the day: Promises I should never have made in the first place are better off broken than kept.

Week Eleven ***Some Tests of*** Exodus 20:1-17
Day Four ***Right and Wrong*** Matthew 7:12
John 13:34, 35

When immobilized by loss, we may be unable to decide anything. This can keep us from acting impulsively, but we can't just drift. Decisions must be made. How do we make them most wisely?

There are no fail-safe routes to correct decisions, but there are some tests of right and wrong to which we can submit our options for review. Here are three for today:

1. Is a contemplated action in accord with the Ten Commandments?
2. Is it in harmony with the Golden Rule: "Do unto others as you would have them do unto you"?
3. Is it affirmed by Jesus' new commandment: "Love one another as I have loved you"?

These tests relate especially to moral decisions and include choices concerning our treatment of others, the relationships we establish and the way we spend our time and money. A vow to never forgive, or to smear someone's reputation, would fail these tests, as would behaviors that seek companionship at any price.

The Ten Commandments, the Golden Rule and Jesus' command to love as he loves are not given to decrease our happiness. They are God's gifts for our good and are guaranteed in the long run to limit our misery and increase our joy.

Prayer: Thank you, God, for your daily guidance. Show us the wisdom of treating ourselves and others with love and respect and give us the strength to act accordingly. In Jesus' name. Amen

Thought for the day: Sinful behavior is not just bad — it's bad for us and bad for others.

Consider the Consequences

Proverbs 16:25
Luke 14:28-32
Romans 13:8-10

Here are four tests of right and wrong that invite us to consider the consequences of our behavior.

1. Will my contemplated action be hurtful or helpful to myself and others?
2. Will I be grateful tomorrow if this deed is done today?
3. Ten years from now will I be thankful to have done what I am thinking of doing today?
4. Will I be pleased to tell my grandchildren about it?

These tests relate not only to issues with moral implications, but also to questions such as "Where should I live?", "Should I marry again?", or "What kind of car should I buy?", which are less directly ethical in nature.

An insurance check may prompt a trip to Hawaii or purchase of a new car, but asking how these actions will look in retrospect may suggest more conservative spending. The solace of a stiff drink may tempt us to drown our sorrows in alcohol, but then we imagine ourselves becoming alcoholics and wisely resolve to never use alcohol as a drug and to never drink when we "need a drink."

Although we cannot be certain today of how we will feel tomorrow, our imagining the consequences of today's deeds helps us be more objective in our decision making. We are free to choose, we are not free to choose the consequences of our choosing. Imagining those consequences helps us remember that short-term delight may result in long-term misery and that short-term suffering may lead to long-term joy.

Prayer: O Lord, give us wisdom to see our actions in light of their consequences. Show us the right roads and give us patience and strength to follow them. In Jesus' name. Amen

Thought for the day: I will act today for a better tomorrow.

Proverbs 1:8, 9
A Wider Perspective Proverbs 15:22

These tests of right and wrong help us see our choices in light of the wisdom of others.

1. Is my contemplated action something I would be glad to have printed in the newspaper?
2. Is it something I'd like those I most respect to know about?
3. Is it something the person I mourn would want me to do?
4. Would the world be better, or worse, if everyone were to behave as I am thinking of acting?

Our decisions should not be dictated by public opinion or even by respected friends and family members. But consultation with an objective outsider helps us see things that we, in emotional distress, may fail to consider. Don't ask anyone to tell you what to do, but rather invite a wise person to help you discover and evaluate alternative courses of action.

It often helps to list the pros and cons of a contemplated action and then to weigh the significance of each factor. One major benefit may outweigh a dozen minor negatives and vice versa. We are ultimately responsible for our own decisions but conversation with the living and remembrance of the wisdom of the dead can help us choose more wisely.

Prayer: Thank you, Lord, for the guidance of other people. Give us openness to listen and to learn. At the same time, give us courage to stand up to others who would wrongly run our lives. In Jesus' name. Amen

Thought for the day: "Two heads are (usually) better than one."

In the Context of Grace

At best, we will make some wrong decisions. The most carefully-calculated choice may turn out to be a mistake. Some, for example, have followed conservative counsel and placed life savings and insurance funds in the guaranteed security of a bank account, only to see their savings depleted by inflation. Others who purchased stocks or mutual funds as a hedge against inflation have sometimes watched their investments decline so much that they wished their money had been in a bank or even under the mattress.

We can't be certain of the wisdom of any complex decision. Even as we choose, we pray "O Lord, this way seems best. If it's right, sustain me; if it's wrong, correct me and bring some good out of it."

Trusting in the forgiveness and creative possibilities of God's power does not reduce our responsibility for careful decision-making, but it keeps our choices in the context of God's grace. Whatever we decide, we trust that God is with us, working to bring good out of both our wisdom and our folly. It may be true, as Paul Sponheim has said, that "God can bring more good out of good than God can bring out of evil" so we best not presume on God's providence. But we do have the assurance in Christ that our worst mistakes do not stop God from loving us and from opening new possibilities for beginning again.

Prayer: O Lord, give us wisdom to make right decisions and lead us beyond the wrong choices into new beginnings. In Jesus' name. Amen

Thought for the day: I will make mistakes, but not the mistake of thinking that my mistakes put me beyond the reach of God's grace.

Day One   *The Pain of Loneliness*

During early days of bereavement, we are the stars of the funeral drama and are often showered with concern. But soon the ritual is past, and we return to the lonely house to face the emptiness alone. When grief results from factors other than death, the helpful religious rituals and community support are usually absent, but the anguish may be as intense.

Feelings of loneliness and relief may, at first, mingle with each other. The agonizing illness is past, the funeral is over, the marital break has been made. But at the same time, there is the terrible void. We may be struck by the frightening realization that this is the first time in our lives that we have ever lived alone. Even when life before separation was intolerable, we had a kind of companionship, and we may now be surprised to pine for one with whom we had such conflict.

Evenings, weekends, and holidays are often especially lonely. We used to talk at supper and do things together in the evening. When we had a fight, we were still together. Now, even after grief subsides, our loneliness may be as painful as ever.

Prayer: O Lord, lead us through this long night into deeper communion with you and with people. Amen

Thought for the day: We people need people.

Week Twelve **Day Two** · *They Don't Understand* · Matthew 26:30-56

Although it is helpful to be with people, we are often reminded that others don't fully understand. But how can they? They are not in our place. We probably don't understand them either. Nobody ever fully understands anyone else. Even in intimacy, we are, in some sense, alone. There is an irreducible loneliness in every life. For all our socializing, we face life and death deeply alone.

So it was for Jesus. He was often in great crowds and was close to his disciples, but he was still profoundly alone. The closest did not understand and, in his hour of crisis, fell asleep. "Could you not watch with me one hour?" (Matthew 26:40) Then, when he was arrested, they abandoned him altogether.

It is painful for us to be alone in our grief and it is also hard for others who seek to give us comfort. They don't know what to say or do. To share another's grief is never easy. This is a difficult time for family and friends, as well as for ourselves; and we, too, will try to understand.

Prayer: O Lord, as we would be understood, help us to understand. Lead us to deeper levels of insight and empathy. In Jesus' name. Amen

Thought for the day: We seek to be understood and to understand.

The Fifth Wheel

When we lose someone with whom we used to share everything, we often also lose our place in the world. We don't belong any more and may feel like a fifth wheel. Couples with whom we shared so much still invite us, but it's not the same. Like the lepers who were shunned by the healthy, we too are reminders of the death and suffering that we all try to avoid.

Although others may be uncomfortable to be with us, our presence may help them be more realistic about the painful facts of life and death. Since no one can escape reality, there is no sense in hiding ourselves to avoid making others feel uneasy. We will endure the pain that we feel and the discomfort we may cause and through it hope for mutual growth and understanding.

We especially thank God for relationships independent of the absent partner. These can often continue much as before. They remind us that we are not to be everything to each other. When we are totally dependent upon someone, we make a "god" of him or her and are setting ourselves up for intense anxiety and loneliness when that relationship ends.

Prayer: Thank you, Lord, for friends who do not fail. Keep us in the company of caring people. In Jesus' name. Amen

Thought for the day: There are places for me, and I will find them.

Week Twelve **The Lonely** Ecclesiastes 3:1-11
Day Four ***Are Not Alone***

We who are lonely have lots of company. Thousands grieve with us today as we share in an experience common to all generations. Our parents and grandparents, all the way back to the beginnings of human history, have traveled this road before us.

We also remember those who have not had a close relationship to lose. I asked a teenage boy, "Who is your best friend?" In reply he took a little radio from his pocket and said, "This is the only friend I've got." His situation is not unique. Others' best friends are people they see on TV.

Had we not loved and been loved, we would have had no love to lose. Had the person we mourn never entered our lives, we should have been spared this grief. But then, think of all the joy we would have missed. Our present anguish is a measure of blessings shared for which we now give thanks through tears. Is it not better to have known this love than to never have loved at all? Therefore, we see our loss of love in the light of lack of love experienced by so many. They survive and carry on; can we do less?

Prayer: O Lord, give us in our loneliness a sense of the vast fellowship of all who suffer. In Jesus' name. Amen

Thought for the day: Millions know the loss or lack of love.

Beware!

When we are lonely, two warnings are in order. Be wary of retreating into isolation, and also of seeking companions with such desperation that we drive people away or get involved in hurtful relationships.

Having felt loss, we are reluctant to experience it again and, to avoid future grief, may shun new relationships. To avoid disappointment we may cease to hope for anything good. We may even feel that it would be disloyal to seek new friends. These thoughts tempt us to live in a world of memories, cut off from people. Such retreat may be necessary for a time, but it can become social suicide. We are created for community and are to "choose life." (Deuteronomy 30:19)

On the other hand, in lonely desperation we may become involved with people who are ill-suited for us. Misery loves company, and some who seem to be understanding of our crisis may not share our basic interests or outlook on life. The best prospects for significant friendship share our view of life and care for our welfare as well as their own. We should especially beware of mistaking pity for love. Pity is a poor basis for either lasting friendship or marriage. Long-lasting, healthy relationships are based on more than feeling sorry for each other.

Prayer: O Lord, save us from either fleeing or frantically pursuing people. Keep us open to life-giving love. Amen

Thought for the day: I will seek friends, but wisely.

In our separations from people we have opportunity to learn new dimensions of communion with God. The old saying is true: "Our extremities are God's opportunities." This does not mean that sad separations are good in themselves, but that God can use them to reveal his presence with us.

Even when his disciples fled, Jesus knew that he was not alone. "You will be scattered . . . and will leave me alone; yet I am not alone, for the Father is with me." (John 16:32) Jesus assures us that God will be with us every moment of time and eternity.

Jesus offers an abiding friendship: "I have called you friends." (John 15:15) Whatever our loss or lack of love, Jesus says "Abide in my love." (John 15:9) Abiding constantly in the friendship of that love, we thankfully sing:

> What a friend we have in Jesus,
> All our sins and griefs to bear! . . .
> Can we find a friend so faithful
> Who will all our sorrows share?

Prayer: O Lord, assure us of your abiding friendship and keep us confident that you will never leave us. In Jesus' name. Amen

Thought for the day: In the company of Christ, we are never alone.

Week Twelve   Philippians 4:4-9
Day Seven   *Serenity in Solitude*   Psalm 51:10-12

It is significant that the English language has two words for being alone: "loneliness" speaks of the pain of separation from those we love; "solitude" tells of meaning and joy experienced in aloneness.

We are created for companionship and grieve the loss and lack of love. We are also created for solitude and need time for quiet reflection and contemplation. Jesus sought renewal in solitude. "After he had dismissed the crowds, he went up on the mountain by himself to pray." (Matthew 14:23)

Sometimes, hours of painful loneliness can be changed into times of serene solitude. Now we have time to ponder and pray and to meet great figures of Scripture, history, and literature. In long night watches a sense of divine presence may flood our lives with "the peace of God, which passes all understanding." (Philippians 4:7) The joy of solitude does not cancel the pain of loneliness, but it does provide a kind of meaning and beauty we may have missed in less lonely times.

Prayer: O Lord, change some of our terrible loneliness into meaningful solitude. In Jesus' name. Amen

Thought for the day: In the grace of God the pain of loneliness can be overcome by the serenity of solitide.

Week Thirteen
Day One

Antidotes
for Self-Pity

1 Kings 19:9-18

It is easy to feel sorry for ourselves. When wronged, why not indulge in a little self-pity? One reason for not doing so is that it does no one any good; self-pity is useless and unattractive. Healthy anger can clear the air and cleanse the psyche; fear may warn of danger — but what good is self-pity? It only keeps us miserable and poisons our relationships.

Like Elijah, we may feel like crawling into a cave to die. But then God asks, "What are you doing here?" (1 Kings 19:9, 13) With Elijah we may reply that we have been misunderstood and mistreated and complain that "I, even I only, am left; and they seek my life, to take it away." (1 Kings 19:10, 14) But the Lord rejects our excuses and, calling us out of self-pity, says in effect, "Stop feeling sorry for yourself. Thousands share your suffering and your faith. I love you and have work for you to do; trust me and get busy caring for others."

Prayer: O Lord, thank you for calling us out of our caves of self-pity. Save us from useless self-preoccupation and give us renewed purposes for living. In Jesus' name. Amen

Thought for the day: I am created for Christ and not for a cave.

Strong treatment is often needed to cure self-pity, and Jesus offers such medicine. A would-be follower asked for time, saying, "Lord, let me first go and bury my father," to which Jesus replied, "Leave the dead to bury their own dead; but as for you, go and proclaim the kingdom of God." (Luke 9:59-60)

It is very difficult for us to "leave the dead" or to "say farewell to those at my house." (Luke 9:61) We try to preserve their presence and may be reluctant to alter the rooms in which they lived or to change anything from the way it was when they were alive. When carried to an extreme, this can turn a home into a museum kept in memory of the dead.

Jesus does not want us to live this way. It is good to treasure mementos of a meaningful relationship, but we are not to be prisoners of the past or live under the lordship of any person, living or dead. Only Christ is Lord, and he says, "No one who puts his hand to the plow and looks back is fit for the kingdom of God." (Luke 9:62) This is strong medicine but we sometimes need to take it.

Prayer: O Lord, shock us out of living in the past and bring us into life now. In Jesus' name. Amen

Thought for the day: In obedience to Jesus, I leave the dead and live for the living.

Remembrance Hebrews 11:1—12:2
and Respect

To "leave the dead" is not to forget them. The Bible remembers the dead and speaks of heroes of faith as a "great cloud of witnesses" (Hebrews 12:1) who are cheering us on in the race of life.

We remember the dead in our prayers. If we prayed for them in life, we cannot suddenly stop doing so; but we can follow Luther's advice that a few prayers are enough. After prayerfully entrusting them to the love of God, we need not prolong our intercessions.

Respect for the dead is shown not only by deeds like visiting the grave, but even more by living in ways that honor the person's memory. We do not show respect by stewing in self-pity. They would not want us to live that way.

A healthy relationship of love actually gives us strength to live without it. The love of parents enables children to live apart from their parents. So also, the love of husband or wife, relative or friend, gives strength to our lives that enables us to go on when they are gone.

Prayer: O Lord, by your love and the love of others, living and dead, enable us now to go on. In Jesus' name. Amen

Thought for the day: By recalling love, we are enabled to live.

One Place of Meeting

Visiting the cemetery, keeping things as they were, and returning to places we shared together are attempts to keep contact with the person we miss so much. These have significance and meaning, but none is a place of meeting.

The Apostle Paul does suggest, however, that there is one place of meeting and that is in the Lord to whom we both belong: "If we live, we live to the Lord, and if we die, we die to the Lord; so whether we live or whether we die we are the Lord's. For to this end, Christ died and lived again that he might be the Lord both of the dead and the living." (Romans 14:7-9)

Although God does not permit communication with the dead, we are not totally out of touch with each other. We are held in love by the same God who is "Lord both of the dead and of the living." (Romans 14:9) As we belong to him, we continue to belong to each other and, in trust of his love, look toward resurrection and greater life together. Separated from each other, we are still united in our Lord.

Prayer: O Lord of the living and the dead, keep us united in your love and bring us by your power to new life in your presence. In Jesus' name. Amen

Thought for the day: We belong to God, and meet in him.

Another antidote for self-pity is to recall those whose suffering is worse than our own. Someone, somewhere, has greater anguish than any other person on earth, and it is unlikely that we are serious candidates for that "honor."

When objective about it, we rightly say, "Things could be worse; many are suffering more than I am." We recall the saying, "I felt sorry for myself because I had no shoes, until I met a person who had no feet." Such thoughts do not reduce our troubles, but they help us see them in better perspective.

Two people describe a glass of water. One says, "It's half empty."; The other says, "It's half full." They are both right; but one sees what is missing, the other what is present. In times of loss, it is well to take stock of what remains.

Our lives may be both half empty and half full. It may even seem unkind to be told to count blessings in times of loss, but we may need to do so. If we can read or hear these lines, we still have our minds and some of our senses for which to be thankful and, when nothing remains but the promises of God in Christ, we still have ground for gratitude.

Prayer: O Lord, as we see our own and others' troubles, help us be more forgetful of self and more caring of others. Amen

Thought for the day: Today I will count my blessings and discount my troubles.

Consider Isaiah 53:1-7
Christ Hebrews 4:14-16; 12:3

We see Jesus as the Suffering Servant who was "despised and rejected by men; a man of sorrows, and acquainted with grief . . . Surely he has borne our griefs and carried our sorrows." (Isaiah 53:3, 4) When in the doldrums of despair and self-pity, we do well to recall the suffering of Jesus who "endured the cross, despising the shame." (Hebrews 12:2) Scripture encourages us to "consider him who endured from sinners such hostility against himself so that you may not grow weary or fainthearted," and we are reminded that "in your struggle against sin, you have not yet resisted to the point of shedding your blood." (Hebrews 12:3, 4)

Our hope in Christ comes from one who has traveled the road of suffering. He knows our anguish and our temptations to self-pity and despair. Jesus is the "one who in every respect has been tempted as we are, yet without sin. Let us then with confidence draw near to the throne of grace, that we may receive mercy and find grace to help in time of need." (Hebrews 4:15-16)

Prayer: O Lord, thank you for caring enough to suffer with and for us. Lead us now through this time of trouble. In Jesus' name. Amen

Thought for the day: Christ is our companion in suffering.

Day Seven   *Gratitude in Grief*

The opposite of self-pity is gratitude. Few contrasts are greater than between the self-pitying and the thankful, and it is amazing that these attitudes seem only indirectly related to situations of life. Some who have everything are bitter, while others who have little are grateful. The difference is in the people, not just their circumstances.

This reminds us of Paul, who said, "I have learned, in whatever state I am, to be content. I know how to be abased, and I know how to abound; in any and all circumstances I have learned the secret of facing plenty and hunger, abundance and want. I can do all things in him who strengthens me." (Philippians 4:11-13)

Paul invites us to give thanks not *for*, but *in*, everything; "*in* everything . . . with thanksgiving let your requests be made known to God." (Philippians 4:6; my emphasis) He can even say, "We rejoice in our sufferings, knowing that suffering produces endurance, and endurance produces character, and character produces hope." (Romans 5:3-4) By itself, suffering often produces bitterness and self-pity. But in the grace of God the curse of sufferings can be transformed into the blessings of endurance, character and hope.

Prayer: O Lord, cleanse us of self-pity and give us continual ground for gratitude. In Jesus' name. Amen

Thought for the day: By the grace of God, gratitude and grief can go together.

Day One   *"How Long, O Lord?"*   Psalm 13:1-6

With the psalmist of old we also cry, "How long, O Lord? . . . How long must I bear pain in my soul, and have sorrow in my heart all the day?" (Psalm 13:1, 2) At times grief subsides and, for a few hours, we feel like our old selves again. But then loss and longing come surging back to make us wonder if we will ever get over it.

Grieving takes time. Recovery is two steps forward, one step back — and often one step forward, two steps back. Like Jacob, we may refuse to be comforted and feel sure that we will go to our graves mourning (Genesis 37:35); but, by the grace of God, our anguish will not last that long. God has kindly given us only a limited capacity to grieve. After awhile, depression begins to lift, tears run out, the ache is less intense, and we begin to think of other things. When this happens, we need not berate ourselves for disloyal forgetfulness, but can welcome healing as the gift of God.

Prayer: O Lord, through however long it takes, give us faith to trust that healing is happening. In Jesus' name. Amen

Thought for the day: Our grief's run out; God's grace does not.

Week Fourteen   ***What***   Ecclesiastes 3:1-15
Day Two   ***Is Expected?***   Deuteronomy 34:5-8

The Bible says that there is "a time to mourn." (Ecclesiastes 3:4) Some societies have had specific periods for grieving. "The people of Israel wept for Moses . . . thirty days; then the days of weeping and mourning for Moses were ended." (Deuteronomy 34:8) Widows and widowers were often expected to mourn for one year. These cultural expectations recognize that grief takes time and that mourners deserve special consideration.

Ancient cultures that prescribed periods of grieving were often equally insistent that mourning come to an end. They often specified that one year was long enough. The person could still grieve in private, but he or she was now expected to return to the normal duties of life and was free to seek new friendships. We can learn from these customs to take time to grieve and also to let our mourning cease so that we can begin again to live and love.

Prayer: O Lord, keep us in grief as long as necessary; bring us out of grief as soon as possible. In Jesus' name. Amen

Thought for the day: "There is a time to weep and a time to laugh; a time to mourn and a time to dance." (Ecclesiastes 3:4)

| Week Fourteen | *"It Came* | 2 Corinthians 4:7—5:5 |
| Day Three | *To Pass"* | Romans 8:18-25 |

Someone picked "It came to pass" as the most help-ful verse in the Bible. This person misunderstood. "It came to pass" is an old way of saying that something happened, but this person thought it meant that troubles do not last forever. While wrong on the text, the mistake captures an insight that is true: our troubles are temporal.

Paul says, "I consider that the sufferings of this present time are not worth comparing with the glory that is to be revealed to us." (Romans 8:18) And again, "We do not lose heart. Though our outer nature is wasting away, our inner nature is being renewed every day. For this slight momentary affliction is preparing us for an eternal weight of glory beyond all comparison." (2 Corinthians 4:16, 17) These promises enabled Paul to say, "We are always of good courage." (2 Corinthians 5:6)

Yet think of what Paul was going through: "We are afflicted in every way, but not crushed; perplexed, but not driven to despair; persecuted for the forsaken; struck down but not destroyed." (2 Corinthians 4:8-9) These burdens were "a slight momentary affliction"? While not slight in themselves, Paul saw them as next to nothing compared with "the glory" to come.

Prayer: O Lord, open our eyes to see temporal troubles in the light of your eternal presence. In Jesus' name. Amen

Thought for the day: Our problems "come to pass." God's presence comes to stay.

We Begin to Live Again

As our broken hearts begin to mend, we may feel like one recovering from long-term illness. The clouds of gloom begin to lift and the world again seems a brighter place. It even may seem like being raised from death to life. With the Apostle Paul we also confess that:

We were so utterly, unbearably crushed that we despaired of life itself. Why, we felt that we had received the sentence of death; but that was to make us rely not on ourselves, but on God who raises the dead; he delivered us from so deadly a peril, and he will deliver us; on him we have set our hope that he will deliver us again.

(2 Corinthians 1:8-10)

Jesus says, "Unless a grain of wheat falls into the earth and dies, it remains alone; but if it dies, it bears much fruit." (John 12:24) This death to self as "god" is the birth of self as an authentic human being. In Christ we die to live. Jesus promises life to come and gives new life today. The eternal life Christ gives is more than a place in heaven; it is new life now, life with an eternal dimension, life lived by the grace of the living God. It is as Paul says: "We were buried therefore with him by baptism into death, so that as Christ was raised from the dead by the glory of the Father, we too might walk in newness of life." (Romans 6:4)

Prayer: Thank you, Lord, for signs of dawn. Open us like flowers to the sunshine of a new day. In Jesus' name. Amen

Thought for the day: We live poorly as make-believe "gods." We live amazingly well as authentic human beings.

Week Fourteen	*New Life*	1 John 3:11-18
Day Five	*With People*	John 3:1-17;
		13:1-17, 34, 35

New life in Christ is new life with God. We are "born of the Spirit." (John 3:6) We are also "born of God." (1 John 4:7) These passages invite us to daily new birth into grace-given, grace-filled life.

New life in Christ is also new life with people. We are to "love one another; even as I have loved you." (John 13:34) As "he laid down his life for us, . . . we ought to lay down our lives for the brethren." (1 John 3:16)

In the intense agony of the initial grief, it is difficult for us to give our attention or our care to anyone or anything beyond the memories and concerns that crowd our minds. But now we begin to see other people again and are enabled to enter their lives with understanding and compassion.

We come out of grief with a deeper sense of how much we need one another. Although fearful that new commitments may lead to more disappointment and grief, we begin to risk ourselves little by little, in new ventures of life together. As we forget ourselves in self-giving concern for others, we enrich their lives and again experience what Jesus promised when he said, "Whoever loses his life for my sake will find it." (Matthew 16:25)

Prayer: O Lord, guide us to the people we need and to the people who need us. In Jesus' name. Amen

Thought for the day: Love gives life and life gives love.

Be Good Mark 12:28-34
To Yourself 1 Corinthians 6:12-20

Having often been urged to be good to others, we may need someone to tell us to be good to ourselves. In grief we sometimes feel guilty for enjoying anything and even for being alive.

However we feel, Jesus says we are to love our neighbors as we love ourselves. That command assumes that we are treating ourselves properly. If we were to treat others as we sometimes treat ourselves, it would hardly be doing them a favor.

We are not our own, but are "bought with a price" and are to "glorify God" in our bodies. (1 Corinthians 6:20) As stewards of life, we are to be good to ourselves and are to take good care of our health and strength. Since life is more than mere existence, it is right for us to spend some time and money on recreation and entertainment. Such refreshment is often more healthful and more economical than the rehabilitation required to recover from neglect of our physical, emotional, mental and spiritual needs. If we are always giving without receiving, we will soon have nothing to give. Our being good to ourselves is one way by which we let God love us.

Prayer: O Lord, give us a healthy sense of self-respect and guide us to be good to ourselves. In Jesus' name. Amen

Thought for the day: Since God loves and is good to me, I will love and be good to myself.

"For the Beauty of the Earth"

We visited together as the spring sun beamed through my study window. For six months he had been numb with grief and depression. The world had seemed black and white. "But now," he said, looking to the sunny window, "I'm coming out of it. I can see the colors again and begin to enjoy a beautiful day."

Our loss has magnified the ugly side of life, but that is not the whole story. As the numbness of sorrow gives way to new awareness, we begin to see beauty again. Our scriptures for today, and lines like these from A. E. Housman, invite us to bask in the beauty of the earth:

> Loveliest of trees, the cherry now
> Is hung with bloom along the bough,
> And stands about the woodland ride
> Wearing white for Eastertide.

> Now, of my threescore years and ten,
> Twenty will not come again,
> And take from seventy springs a score,
> It only leaves me fifty more.

> And since to look at things in bloom
> Fifty springs are little room,
> About the woodlands I will go
> To see the cherry hung with snow.

Prayer: For the beauty of the earth,
For the beauty of the skies,
For the joy of ear and eye,
For the heart's and mind's delight,
Lord of all, to thee we raise
This our hymn of grateful praise. Amen

Thought for the day: "A thing of beauty is a joy forever."

Day One   *"Six Weeks 'Til Frost"*

   Our loss has made us painfully aware of the brevity of life. Words on a graveyard gate speak from the dead to the living: "What you are, we were; what we are, you will be." So, too, these words from long ago:

> The years of our life are threescore years and ten,
>   or even by reason of strength fourscore; . . .
>   they are soon gone, and we fly away . . .
>   So teach us to number our days
> that we may get a heart of wisdom. (Psalm 90:10, 12)

   A little poem by Stephen Vincent Benét, significantly titled "Thirty-Five," shares such wisdom:

> The sun was hot, the sky was bright,
>   And all July was overhead.
> I heard the locusts first that night
>   "Six weeks 'til frost," they said.

"Six weeks 'til frost" — that is the story of life and death. Part of our grief is sadness that we, too, will die.

Prayer: Abide with me; fast falls the eventide;
      The darkness deepens; Lord, with me
         abide! . . .
      Change and decay in all around I see;
      O thou who changest not, abide with me.
      Amen

   Thought for the day: "Today is going to be long, long ago."

As we gain awareness of the shortness of life, every moment becomes more precious and we live with a gift-sense of time. We can no longer plan our years with certainty, for each day is a gift of grace.

To some who are presumptuous, we, too, feel like saying:

> *Come now, you who say, "Today or tomorrow we will go into such and such a town and spend a year there and trade and get gain"; whereas you do not know about tomorrow. What is your life? For you are a mist that appears for a little time and then vanishes. Instead you ought to say, "If the Lord wills, we shall live and we shall do this or that." As it is, you boast in your arrogance. All such boasting is evil. (James 4:13-16)*

Facing this fact may shock us out of the arrogant illusion that "I am the master of my fate, I am the captain of my soul." But it also helps us realize that "my times are in thy hand." (Psalm 31:15) He who keeps time and eternity is also our "keeper." (Psalm 121:5) In him we are safe now and forever.

All this does not say we should have no concern for tomorrow. Planning for tomorrow is a vital part of each day's work, but we do that work with awareness that the present is the only moment in which we ever live.

Prayer: O Lord, give us a gift-sense of life and time. Thank you that our times are in your hands. In Jesus' name. Amen

Thought for the day: Today I will receive each moment as a gift from God.

Many of our dreams won't come true, and some of the work we had hoped to do will never be done. As dreams die and hopes fade, we suffer the frustration of living with unfinished business.

One thing we can learn is to do each day's work one day at a time. Lowell Satre once spoke on "learning to plod." He quoted Jesus: "Behold, I cast out demons and perform cures today and tomorrow, and the third day I finish my course. Nevertheless I must go on my way today and tomorrow and the day following." (Luke 13:32, 33) With Jesus, we walk one step at a time. We won't do everything; but we can do something, and much of it is done in steady plodding.

We also trust others to carry on the work we have begun. "I planted," says Paul. "Apollos watered . . . I laid a foundation, and another man is building upon it." (1 Corinthians 3:6, 10) No one will do exactly what we would have done, but the building will go on.

Above all, we trust this promise: "He who began a good work in you will bring it to completion at the day of Jesus Christ." (Philippians 1:6) Lives cut short by tragedy were not lived in vain. God himself will complete the work begun in them and in us.

Prayer: O Lord, teach us to plod, to trust in others, and, above all, to trust in you to complete your work in us, through us and beyond us.

Thought for the day: "We must work . . . while it is day; night comes, when no one can work." (John 9:4)

To Be A
Person

Roles end. Wives becomes widows, husbands widowers. The married become separated or divorced. When the last parent dies, we join the older generation. Workers become retired or unemployed, the healthy get sick, the young too soon grow old.

If marriage has been everything to us, what is left when marriage ends? Does life die when work is done? We can seek new roles and new work — but when this is impossible, what then?

The challenge is to live as a person rather than a role. We are not just husbands, wives, parents, children, employees, and employers. We are persons created in God's image and have worth apart from our roles. We have names as well as titles. We are Bill or Mary, and not just Mom or Dad, husband or wife, nurse or doctor. We have worth and dignity as persons apart from our roles.

Having wrestled "until the breaking of the day," Jacob got a new name. "Your name shall no more be called Jacob, but Israel." (Genesis 32:28) That meant he was a new person. We come out of our long night of grief missing old roles, but still persons whom God calls by name: "Fear not, for I have redeemed you; I have called you by name, you are mine." (Isaiah 43:1)

Prayer: O Lord, as we lose our titles, give us new respect for our names. In Jesus' name. Amen

Thought for the day: By the grace of God I will live as a person and not just as a role.

Week Fifteen   *"You*   1 Corinthians 3:21-32
Day Five   *Are Christ's"*   Deuteronomy 33:27

One of the most vital questions we can be asked is "To whom do you belong?" Paul answers, "You are not your own; you were bought with a price." (1 Corinthians 6:19, 20) and again, "All things are yours, whether Paul or Apollos or Cephas or the world or life or death or the present or the future, all are yours; and you are Christ's and Christ is God's." (1 Corinthians 3:21-23)

We don't belong to Paul or anyone else, living or dead. Nor are the world, life, death, present, or future our masters. We belong to Christ who alone is Lord of our lives. No one and no thing is to rule over us. In Christ even death is no more master. By the power of God, "the last enemy" has been conquered. "Christ being raised from the dead will never die again; death no longer has dominion over him." (Romans 6:9)

The events of every present moment unfold beneath Christ's reign. Held tightly to him, we live a bit loosely with everything else. Marriage, family, the world, the present, the future, even death — all are temporal. Beyond all these, we belong to God, who is eternal. God alone is worthy of our total loyalty, trust and commitment.

Prayer: O Lord, save us from being overinvested in things temporal and underinvested in things eternal. In Jesus' name. Amen

Thought for the day: I will say "good-bye" to the people and things of this world. I will never say "good-bye" to God.

Week Fifteen   *Look For the*   Revelation 8:7-17
Day Six   *Open Door*   Luke 18:24-30

When the world closes in on us, there often seems nowhere to turn: but in the grace of God, at least one door is always open. Like those to whom John wrote, we "have but little power." But we, too, have this promise: "Behold, I have set before you an open door, which no one is able to shut." (Revelation 3:8) In Christ the door of grace is always open. Jesus' open arms welcome us to the embrace of his love. And then having received us to himself, Jesus, in effect, turns us around and says, "Look! There is someone who needs you. Go now and meet that need."

The promise of an open door encourages us to think of the possibilities as well as the problems of life. This does not mean that we should adopt naive optimism or pretend that if we just try hard enough we will triumph over everything. Many things are frankly impossible for us. But "what is impossible with [people] is possible with God." (Luke 18:27)

A young boy tried to move a large rock in the backyard. After giving up, he told his father, "I've tried everything; it can't be moved." His father replied, "You haven't tried me." They went out together and moved the rock. If we think we've tried everything it may be time to call on our Heavenly Father. What is impossible for us is possible for God.

Prayer: Thank you, Lord, for open doors to your love and to people who need our care. In Jesus' name. Amen

Thought for the day: God's power exceeds my problems.

With the Luke 10:25-37
Compassion of Christ Col. 3:12-17

As grace heals our bitterness and resentment, we grow in compassion for others. We sense the immense suffering around us and the importance of caring for one another.

Jesus tells of one who came to a man beaten by the side of the road, "and when he saw him, he had compassion." (Luke 10:33) That good Samaritan invites us to live with the compassion of Christ, who sends each of us to "go and do likewise." (Luke 10:37)

Having suffered ourselves, we realize that others, too, may be having a tough struggle. When they are irritable, it may be a sign of their anguish. Our miseries have made it hard for others to live with us; their pains of mind and body may make it hard for us to live with them. When this happens we need to:

Put on then, as God's chosen ones, holy and beloved, compassion, kindness, lowliness, meekness and patience, forbearing one another and, if one has a complaint against another, forgiving each other; as the Lord has forgiven you, so you also must forgive. And above all these things put on love which binds everything together in perfect harmony.
(Colossians 3:12-14)

Prayer: O Lord, thank you for those who have been kind to us. Give us kindness and patience to deal gently with people in pain. In Jesus' name. Amen

Thought for the day: Instead of condemning, I will seek to understand and to show compassion.

Sing a
New Song

Our moods need not match our miseries. The first disciples had both great trouble and much joy. Paul and Silas were beaten and thrown "into the inner prison" with "their feet in the stocks"; yet they "were praying and singing hymns to God." (Acts 16:24-25) A song to God while in stocks in prison! How can this be? They sang to God, whose presence was more real than their pains or problems.

We may be confined to a prison of sorrow or sickness, but God is with us. His presence and promises let us sing of life in the face of death.

Paul and Silas were not so sick that they enjoyed being miserable. They had great trouble, but they had a greater God. Perhaps they sang:

> O sing to the Lord a new song,
> for he has done marvelous things! (Psalm 98:1)

Prayer: O Lord, give us a new song in our hearts — a song of your love and victory. In Jesus' name. Amen

Thought for the day: "This is my Father's world;
Why should my heart be sad?
The Lord is King, let the heavens ring;
God reigns let the earth be glad!"

A Time To Laugh

Some think a funeral should be only a joyful celebration and that tears have no place in a Christian life. Yet, "Jesus wept" (John 11:35) and, in doing so, blesses our tears and assures us that it is right to grieve.

There is "a time to weep," but there is also "a time to laugh." (Ecclesiastes 3:4) As some condemn Christians who cry, others judge those who laugh. Years ago one pious family had this rule: "It's all right to smile, but it's a sin to laugh." This is sick religion. In some families that sad rule seems still to be in effect. We may even impose it on ourselves. To laugh may seem disrespectful and a sign that we are not grieving as we should.

There are times when tears and laughter are out of place, but our more common danger is that both be wrongly suppressed. They are unique human gifts, given by a God of love to bless his children. When something is sad or touching, we need not be ashamed to cry. When something is funny, we can laugh, assured of God's blessing.

Life is a rhythm of joy and sorrow, laughter and tears. "Blessed are you that weep now," said Jesus, "for you shall laugh." (Luke 6:21b) There are times for tears and times for laughter. It is good to cry and good to laugh.

Prayer: Thank you, Lord, for tears and laughter. By your grace, enable us to weep and to laugh. In Jesus' name. Amen

Thought for the day: Tears tell of my sadness, laughter of my joy.

The Unshakeable Hebrews 11:8-10;
Kingdom 12:25-29; 13:1-9

Our foundations of life have been shaken. We wondered if we would survive. Now we can begin to look back with gratitude and some amazement to have done as well as we have.

Many factors have sustained us. We thank God for the resiliency built into our lives. Friends and family have helped. Things to do have kept us occupied and useful. But above all, we have been sustained by the grace of God. Like Abraham, we ventured into the unknown, "looking forward to the city which has foundations, whose builder and maker is God." (Hebrews 11:10)

We have discovered an unshakeable foundation for faith in Jesus Christ, who in steadfast love has proved to be "the same yesterday and today and forever." (Hebrews 13:8) Trusting him, we join in this great "therefore" of thanksgiving and praise: "Therefore, let us be grateful for receiving a kingdom that cannot be shaken, and thus let us offer to God acceptable worship, with reverence and awe." (Hebrews 12:28) In thankful trust we sing:

> On Christ the solid rock I stand;
> All other ground is sinking sand . . .
> When all around my soul gives way,
> He then is all my hope and stay.

Prayer: O Lord, other foundations tremble, but we set out trust upon the rock of your love and power. Thank you. In Jesus' name. Amen

Thought for the day: "I will never fail you nor forsake you." (Hebrews 13:5)

Week Sixteen

Day Four

"Thanks Be To God"

1 Corinthians 15:42-58

Psalm 100:1-5

Psalm 103:1-22

Psalm 121:1-8

The true mark of joy is gratitude. Though often through tears, we give thanks to God and, with that gratitude, tell of joy in the midst of sorrow. We stress again that this is thanks *to God* and not *for trouble or tragedy.* With the Apostle Paul we rejoice that "Death is swallowed up in victory" and go on to share this triumphant affirmation of trust and thanksgiving:

> Death is swallowed up in victory
> O Death where is thy victory?
> O Death where is thy sting?

"The sting of death is sin, and the power of sin is the law. But thanks be to God who gives us the victory through our Lord Jesus Christ." (1 Corinthians 15:54-57)

How different our lives would be if we lived every moment with such confidence and gratitude! In spite of trouble and sorrow, life would be perpetual joy, with strength and hope abounding. Such ecstasy may come, but it also goes. Our faith falters, our hopes rise and fall. Still, whatever our moods, God calls us again to thankful trust and joyful hope. God's grace is solid ground for gratitude.

Prayer: "Bless the Lord, O my soul, and forget not all his benefits." In Jesus' name. Amen

Thought for the day: Grace gives gratitude, and gratitude tells of joy.

Week Sixteen	*"Hans Had*	2 Corinthians 5:1-15
Day Five	*a Great God!"*	Psalm 145:1-21
		Psalm 150:1-6

As family and friends walked slowly from the open grave, one was heard to say, "Hans had a great God." That comes close to saying it all. It tells nothing about what Hans looked like or what he did and yet it tells the one thing that really matters: "Hans had a great God"! Will each of us be remembered in a similar way? In the grace of God such remembrance is possible for each of us. We don't need a special talent to achieve it. All we need to do is to let God be God for us and he will take care of the rest. This is the God of whom the psalmist wrote in these words of praise:

> Great is the Lord, and greatly to be praised, and his great-ness is unsearchable . . . the Lord is gracious and merciful, slow to anger and abounding in steadfast love. The Lord is good to all and his compassion is over all that he has made . . . The Lord is faithful in all his words, and gracious in all his deeds. The Lord upholds all who are falling, and raises up all who are bowed down. (Psalm 145:3, 8, 9, 13, 14)

Exalted as they are, the psalmist's words are under-statement. We cannot exaggerate or overstate the great-ness and goodness of God. We cannot trust God too much or praise God too highly. The greatest hymns of praise are all understatements. All we can do, and all we need to do, is to let God be for us the great God that he is.

Prayer: With wonder we praise you, O Lord; may all the universe sing of your glory. In Jesus' name. Amen

Thought for the day: "God is great, and God is good."

Blessings Beyond Belief

The greatness of God is not limited by the smallness of our faith. When the disciples first heard of Jesus' resurrection, "these words seemed to them an idle tale, and they did not believe them." (Luke 24:12) It was simply too good to be true. Assurance of his living presence soon became conviction for their lives, but it was at first beyond their capacity to believe.

We too find some blessings beyond belief. They seem too good to be true. There is reality in these feelings. God "is able to do far more abundantly than all that we ask or think." (Ephesians 3:20) We haven't the capacity of imagination or intelligence to comprehend the possibilities of the power of God. "As the heavens are higher than the earth, so are my ways higher than your ways and my thoughts than your thoughts." (Isaiah 55:9)

As he did with the disciples, God seeks to enlarge our capacity to believe. God isn't finished with us yet and has many surprises to reveal. "No eye has seen, nor ear heard, nor heart of man conceived, what God has prepared for those who love him." (1 Corinthians 2:9) Having been surprised by God's love in Jesus, we dare believe that present blessings are but the beginning of blessings yet to be.

Prayer: O Lord, enlarge our faith to match your power. In Jesus' name. Amen

Thought for the day: God can do far more than we can believe.

"The Best Is Yet To Be"

Robert Browning wrote, "Grow old along with me! The best is yet to be." Jesus invites us to trust that to be true. Whatever has been, he bids us look to a day when it will be said:

> *Behold, the dwelling of God is with men. He will dwell with them, and they shall be his people, and God himself will be with them; he will wipe away every tear from their eyes, and death shall be no more, neither shall there be mourning, nor crying nor pain any more, for the former things have passed away.* (Revelation 21:3, 4)

In Christ we look toward fuller life beyond these years, but God promises new life now as well as then. In Christ we dare believe that we "shall see the goodness of the Lord in the land of the living!" (Psalm 27:13) The years remaining may be even better than those having been. This hope is no insult to the person for whom we mourn; it is rather a compliment to God, who wills fulness of life for the bereaved as for all his children.

In Christ we are enabled to live with what someone has called "future in our minds." Whatever our past or our present, the pilgrimage of these days is but the beginning of the best that's yet to be.

Prayer: For the good that has been and the best yet to be, we give you thanks, O Lord. In Jesus' name. Amen

Thought for the day: By the promises of God I will live with future in my mind.

A Blessing for Every Day of Every Week to Come

Sunday: The Lord bless you and keep you:
The Lord make his face to shine upon you,
and be gracious unto you:
The Lord lift up his countenance upon
you, and give you peace. (Numbers 6:24-26)

Monday: May the God of hope fill you with all joy and peace in believing, so that by the power of the Holy Spirit you may abound in hope.
(Romans 15:13)

Tuesday: The grace of the Lord Jesus Christ and the love of God
and the fellowship of the Holy Spirit be with you all. (2 Corinthians 13:14)

Wednesday: Now to him who by the power at work within us is
able to do far more abundantly than all that we ask or think, to him be
glory in the church and in Christ Jesus to all generations, forever and
ever. Amen (Ephesians 3:20, 21)

Thursday: Now may the God of peace who brought again from the
dead our Lord Jesus, the great shepherd of the sheep, by the blood of
the eternal covenant, equip you with everything good that you may do
his will, working in you that which is pleasing in his sight, through Jesus
Christ; to whom be glory for ever and ever. Amen (Hebrews 13:20, 21)

Friday: After you have suffered a little while, the God of all grace,
who has called you to his eternal glory in Christ, will himself restore,
establish, and strengthen you. To him be the dominion for ever and ever.
Amen (1 Peter 5:10, 11)

Saturday: Now to him who is able to keep you from falling and
to present you without blemish before the presence of his glory with rejoicing, to the only God, our Savior through Jesus Christ our Lord, be
glory, majesty, dominion, and authority, before all time and now and
forever. Amen (Jude 24, 25)